ALSO BY RICHARD H. PFEIFFER

Real Solution Anger Control Workbook

Real Solution Assertiveness Workbook

Real Solution Anxiety/Panic Workbook

Real Solution Binge/Compulsive Eating Workbook

For information contact:

Growth Publishing
750 Columbus Ave Suite 9S
New York, NY 10025
212-749-3684
http://www.growthgroups.com
growth@growthgroups.com

CREATING REAL RELATIONSHIPS

Overcoming the Power of Difference and Shame

Richard H Pfeiffer

GROWTH PUBLISHING
DIVISION OF GROWTH CENTRAL, LLC
750 COLUMBUS AVENUE SUITE 9S
NEW YORK, NY 10025
212-749-3684
http://growthgroups.com
growth@growthgroups.com

COPYRIGHT © 1999 RICHARD H PFEIFFER

Printed in the United States of America
-ALL RIGHTS RESERVED-

NO PART OF THIS BOOK MAY BE REPRODUCED OR TRANSMITTED IN ANY FORM OR BY ANY MEANS, ELECTRONIC OR MECHANICAL, INCLUDING PHOTOCOPYING, RECORDING, OR BY ANY INFORMATION STORAGE AND RETRIEVAL SYSTEM, WITHOUT PERMISSION IN WRITING FROM THE PUBLISHER

Growth Publishing
A Division of Growth Central LLC
750 Columbus Ave. Suite 9S, New York, NY 10025

PRINTED IN THE UNITED STATES OF AMERICA

First Printing
March 2000

Library of Congress Cataloguing-in-Publication Data

Pfeiffer, Richard.
   Creating real relationships : overcoming the power of difference and shame / Richard Pfeiffer.
     1st ed.
     P. cm.
     ISBN 1893505138
     Includes index.

     1. Interpersonal relations. 2. Interpersonal conflict. 3. Anger. 4. Shame. I Title.

HM132.P44 2000   158.2
                    QB199-1699

To the memory of my mother and father

Elsa and Richard Pfeiffer

Contents

Preface
Author's Note on Special Use of Words

Part One: Why Are So Few Relationships Real?

Chapter 1: Introduction and Self-Assessments 1
Who Is *Creating Real Relationships* For? 3
What Is the Self? 4
Basic Assumptions About Human Development 4
What Is a Real Relationship? 5
False Self / Real Self Criteria Table 8
Working Individually or Together 9
Assessing Your Emotional Needs 9
Emotional Needs Assessment Form 10
Assessing Your Relationship Problems 12
Relationship Problems Assessment Form 12
Getting Started Building Your Skills 14
Clarifying Expectations 14

Chapter 2: Overcoming the Power of Difference 15
Fantasy and Disenchantment 15
The "No Difference" Fantasy 19
Attraction and Difference 21
Emotional Need Deficits 23
Projective Identification 22
Complementarity 25
Spirituality 27
Spiritual Aspect of Humanity 28
Spiritual Aspect of Humility 28
Spiritual Aspect of Gratitude 28
Spiritual Aspect of Grace 28
Spiritual Aspect of Realness 28
Spiritual Aspect of Meditation 29

Contents

Chapter 3: Overcoming the Power of Shame *31*
Shame as an Inevitable Human Experience *31*
Healthy and Unhealthy Shame *32*
Shame and Relationships *33*
Defenses Against Feeling Shame *34*
Denial *35*
Withdrawal *36*
Perfectionism *37*
Arrogance *38*
Creating a Self-Centered Universe *39*
Rage *39*
Chronic Shame is Relentless and Devastating *41*
Shaming Yourself Excessively *41*
Shame and the Fear of Abandonment *42*
"I Will Be Whatever You Want Me to Be" *42*
Self-Sabotage *43*
Self-Abuse *43*
Self-Neglect *43*
The Tendency to Humiliate Others *44*
Compulsive/Addictive Behaviors *44*
Have Patience: Healing Shame Is a Process *45*
Stage 1: Understand and Accept Your Shame *45*
Become Fully Aware of Your Shame *46*
Explore Your Defenses Against Shame *47*
Explore the Sources of Your Shame *48*
Explore Your Shaming Relationships *48*
Accept Your Shame as Part of the Human Condition *49*
Stage 2: Take Positive Action *50*
Get Help—You Don't Have to Do This Alone *50*
Challenge the Shame *51*
Heal the Shame from Your Family of Origin *51*
Exploring the Past not Getting Stuck in It *52*
Decode Deficiency Messages Received from Your Family *52*
Grieve Your Life Losses Resulting from These Messages *53*
Challenge Old Deficiency Messages *53*
Challenge Your Behavior *54*
Return "Borrowed" Shame *55*

Contents

Part Two: Key Skills for Creating Real Relationships

Chapter 4: Developing Assertiveness Skills 59
Three Basic Types of Communication 59
Assertive Communication 59
Aggressive Communication 60
Passive Communication 61
The Principles of Assertive Communication 61
Assertive Rights 62
Distorted Beliefs versus Assertive Rights Table 63
Confront Your Fears of Being Assertive 66
Criticism as Manipulation 67
Assertive Approaches for Dealing with Criticism 68
Acknowledgment 68
Sorting 69
Agreement in Part 70
Agreement in Principle 70
Agreement in Probability 70
Clarification 71
The Content-to-Process Shift 72
The Broken-Record Approach 73
Slowing It Down 74
Stating Your Position 74
Active Listening 76
Taking Turns Expressing and Listening 77
Making a Relationship Compromise 78
Saying No and Sharing Negative Feelings 79

Contents

Chapter 5: Overcoming Your Anger *83*
   What Is Anger? *83*
   Angry Feelings as a Process *84*
   Angry Feelings Are Different from Aggressive Actions... *85*
   Impulse Beliefs *86*
   Basic Mistrust *86*
   Shoulds *87*
   The Fantasy of Entitlement *88*
   The Fantasy of Unconditional Correctness *88*
   Exaggeration Words *89*
   Shaming Statements *90*
   Dealing with Anger: Coping Works Better Than Shaming... *90*
   Venting Is Not Ultimately Effective *91*
   Calm Yourself with Muscle Relaxation *91*
   Calm Yourself with Visualization *93*
   Self-Talk Phrases for Angry Moments *94*
   Healthy Separateness *95*
   Expressing Limits: Saying No *96*

Chapter 6: Overcoming Your Partner's Anger *99*
   How to Handle Several Types of Angry, Shaming Behavior *99*
   Depriving You of an Emotional Need *100*
   The Story of Narcissus *100*
   Applying Guilt *101*
   Invalidating Your Needs *102*
   Threatening to Leave *104*
   Threatening Harmful Consequences *105*
   Calling You Names or Putting You Down *105*
   Saying Yes but Meaning No *107*
   Ask for a Healthy Time-Out *108*

Contents

Chapter 7: Overcoming Your Anxiety .... *...111*
Anxiety Threatens Real Relationships .... *...111*
Early Signs of Anxiety .... *...113*
The Anxiety Table .... *...113*
External Causes of Anxiety .... *...114*
Parents Who Were Overly Critical .... *...114*
Families with Emotional Insecurity and Dependency .... *...114*
Cumulative Stress .... *...114*
Internal Causes of Anxiety .... *...115*
Anxious Distorted-Belief Phrases .... *...115*
Pushing Down Feelings .... *...116*
Inadequate Assertive Communication Skills .... *...116*
Inadequate Self-Care Skills .... *...116*
Driven Lifestyle .... *...117*
Inadequate Life Purpose .... *...117*
Poor Nutrition and Smoking .... *...118*
Skills for Overcoming Your Anxiety .... *...118*
Relaxation .... *...119*
Depth Breathing .... *...120*
Physical Exercise .... *...121*
Time Management and Organization .... *...123*
List Jobs and Their Priorities .... *...123*
Organize Your Finances and Mail .... *...123*
Keep a Journal .... *...124*
Organize and Label Your Belongings .... *...124*
Use Driving Time Wisely .... *...125*
Organize Birthdays and Anniversaries .... *...125*
Social Support .... *...126*
Withdrawal from High-Anxiety Situations .... *...128*
Redirecting Attention .... *...129*
Affirmations to Reduce Anxiety .... *...129*

Contents

Chapter 8: Overcoming Distorted Beliefs .... *...133*
Distorted Beliefs Harm Real Relationships .... *...133*
"All or Nothing" Thinking .... *...134*
Shoulds .... *...134*
Catastrophizing .... *...134*
Overgeneralizing .... *...134*
Minimizing/Magnifying .... *...135*
Taking It Personally .... *...135*
Affective (Feelings) Reasoning .... *...136*
Ignoring Coping Abilities .... *...136*
Tunnel Visioning .... *...136*
Impulsive Interpretation .... *...136*
Labeling .... *...137*
Mind Reading .... *...137*
Typical Distorted-Belief Phrases .... *...139*
Distorted-Belief Personality Structures .... *...141*
The Pessimist .... *...141*
The Faultfinder .... *...141*
The Victim .... *...142*
The Perfectionist .... *...142*
Adjusting Distorted-Belief Phrases .... *...143*
Become Aware of Situations .... *...143*
Explore Yourself .... *...143*
Relax or Distract Yourself .... *...144*
Record the Distorted-Belief Phrases .... *...144*
Confront the Distorted-Belief Phrases .... *...145*
Affirmations for Replacing Distorted Beliefs .... *...145*

Contents

Chapter 9: Mastering Basic Conflict Resolution ...147
Why Does Conflict Occur? ...147
Lack of Communication ...148
Lack of Effective Leadership or Decision Making ...148
Value Conflicts ...148
Gender Role Differences ...149
Low Productivity ...149
Change and Transitions ...150
Unresolved Baggage ...150
Distorted Beliefs About Conflict ...151
Destructive Patterns ...151
Conflict Resolution Styles ...152
Denial or Avoidance of the Conflict ...152
Giving In Rather Than Confronting the Conflict ...152
One Partner Getting Angry and Blaming the Other ...152
Seeking an Innovative, Fair, Optimal Solutions ...152
Basic Conflict Resolution Method ...153
Recognize Conflict Issues ...153
Appropriate Time and Place to Discuss the Issues ...153
Treat Each Other with Respect ...153
Listen Carefully ...154
Focus on Emotions ...154
Verbalize the Conflict Issues ...154
Identify Your Share of the Problem ...155
Recognize and Identify Optional Solutions ...156
Choose a Mutually Acceptable Solution ...157
Before Working Through a Conflict with Your Partner ...157

Contents

Chapter 10: Learning Direct Communication Skills .... *...159*
Crucial to Real Relationships .... *...159*
Communication Experience Table .... *...160*
Direct Communication: Skills and Healthy Dynamics .... *...161*
Attention .... *...161*
Listening .... *...162*
Respect .... *...163*
Empathy .... *...164*
Acceptance .... *...166*
Assertiveness .... *...167*
Self-Disclosure .... *...168*
Cooperation .... *...168*
Intimacy .... *...169*
Emotional Support .... *...170*
Compatibility .... *...171*
Barriers to Direct Communication .... *...173*
Playing Games .... *...173*
Colluding .... *...173*
Distorted Listening .... *...174*
Defensiveness .... *...174*
Self-Absorption .... *...175*
Levels of Emotional Expressiveness .... *...175*
Partners Who Are More Emotionally Expressive............... *...175*
Partners Who Are Less Emotionally Expressive................ *...177*

Contents

Chapter 11: Learning the Art of Real Listening ...*179*
Barriers to Real Listening ...*179*
Judgment and Critical Feelings ...*180*
Mind Wandering ...*180*
Fixing and Giving Advice ...*180*
The Need to Be Right ...*180*
Shifting the Focus ...*180*
Pacifying ...*180*
Reading Your Partner's Mind ...*181*
Thinking About What You Will Say Next ...*181*
Selective Listening ...*181*
Real Listening ...*181*
Summary ...*182*
Clarification ...*182*
Process ...*182*
Effective Body Language ...*183*
Empathy ...*183*
Reaching for Information ...*184*
Validation ...*185*
Conclusion ...*186*

Appendix: A Brief Technical Look at Shame ...*189*
Index ...*197*

Preface

This book carries with it the promise of hope: the hope that relationships can encourage, nurture, and support the development of the real self. *Creating Real Relationships* is the result of twenty years of conversation with extraordinary men and women. Under the outward roles of therapist and client, student and teacher, clergyperson and layperson, or colleague and colleague—many individuals have made a positive impact on this work. I want to express my gratitude to all who have influenced this book.

Difference and shame are underlying dynamics that often determine whether a relationship heals or wounds the partners. Shame in relationships has the effect of driving down a partner's real self. Shame steals energy, optimism, and excitement long after its initial pain. Nevertheless, the partner whose face flushes with shame is also one who wants and needs to learn how to hold his or her head up in calm dignity and realistic pride. The message of hope that lies hidden in every moment of the creation of real relationships is that miracles can happen if you work hard for them.

I am very grateful for the positive response from all those who have read and worked with the *Real Solution Anger Control Workbook, Real Solution Assertiveness Workbook, Real Solution Anxiety/Panic Workbook*, and the *Real Solution Binge/Compulsive Eating Workbook*. It has been out of this experience and my work with hundreds of couples and families that I have ventured to offer *Creating Real Relationships*.

I first and foremost want to thank my beloved wife, Anita Bohensky, Ph.D., for the support and love that have truly been the catalysts for *Creating Real Relationships,* both literally and figuratively. Her caring and thoughtful way has enlightened me about mutuality, realness, and overcoming the forces of *distorted beliefs,* shame, and difference. I would also like to thank Janet Frick and Sara Pfeiffer for both their support and editing skills.

I am grateful to my colleagues at the Creative Living Counseling Center for their sharing of themselves and their understanding of this work that we do, especially Dr. Dan Bottorff; Dr. Marilyn Batchelder; Dr. James Wyrtzen; Dr. Gretchen Janssen; Elizabeth Ehling, M.Div.; Shirley Gilliam, M.Div.; Marcia Wyrtzen, L.C.S.W.; Constance Ritzler, M.A.; Dr. Yvonne Martinez Thorne; Dr. Leo Samouilidis; and of course Kathy Corniotes.

I would also like to acknowledge those at Blanton-Peale Graduate Institute who have certainly influenced this work, including Dr. Wilbert Sykes; Dr. Bert Weinblatt; Dr. Herb Rabin; Dr. Margaret Kornfeld; Dr. John McNeill; Dr. James Murphy; Dr. Dustin Nichols; Steve Prichard, M.Div.; Dr. Robert Thorne; Carroll Arkema, M.Div; and Charles Lindner, M.Div. All were helpful in my beginning work with relationship.

I would like to acknowledge those with whom I connected at Drew University School of Theology and who have influenced my work, including Dr. Thomas Oden, Dr. Nelson Thayer, Dr. Arthur Pressley, and Dr. Charles Rice.

Richard H Pfeiffer, MDiv., CGP
Director, Growth Central
New York, NY
www.growthgroups.com

AUTHOR'S NOTE ON SPECIAL USE OF WORDS

A few of the most important terms in this book are familiar words used with very specific, less familiar meanings. These terms appear in *italic* the first time they are used. If the word is not defined the first time it is used, it is also italicized when it is defined.

To avoid possible confusion, here is a list of them and where each is defined:

	Defined
attunement	14
complementarity	16
difference	12
distorted belief	35 and 72
false self	10
impulse beliefs	47
process	97
real, realness	18
real relationship	4
real self	5
self	3
self-talk	47
shame	19
shaming relationship	18
summary	97

PART ONE

WHY ARE SO FEW RELATIONSHIPS REAL?

Chapter 1

Introduction and Self-Assessments

I have often thought that the best way to define a man's character would be to seek out the particular mental or moral attitude in which, when it came upon him, he felt himself most deeply and intensely active and alive. At such a moment there is a voice inside which speaks and says: "This is the real me!"
William James ... letter to his wife, 1878

Human relationships are a reservoir of great joy on one hand and deepest pain on the other. Love begins with both dreams and fantasy: the hope of being understood, known, and truly accepted; the hope of being safe and making another safe, of belonging; the hope of deep passion; the hope of a lasting and transforming bond. But hope collides with the realities of love. Because any two partners are going to have different needs, anger eventually results. Judgments erode away the once flowing acceptance, and loneliness seeps into increasingly distant lives.

Partners who make a *real relationship* work have certain skills. Couples who know and practice core interpersonal skills form relationships that endure, deepen, and grow. That's the good news, because you can decide to learn new skills by learning and practicing.

This book will help you develop and hone the skills you need to create and maintain a real relationship and to keep love alive. The focus is on action and change by using skills and concepts for overcoming the underlying dynamics of *difference* and *shame*. This means that you can't just passively sit and read. You'll need to get involved by risking new behaviors and trying new responses. It will take patience and persistence, and sometimes courage. But your hopes and dreams are worth the effort. A real relationship will not happen by chance or because you understand more, or your partner undergoes some surprise change, but because you and your partner have worked to become more skillful at being a couple.

More good news is that you do not need to read the entire book. Partners need to concentrate on different skills. Each chapter in Part Two contains the essentials of what you will need to learn for a particular skill. You may choose the specific skills you want to learn and skip the rest. The result is that you can start right now to relate differently to your partner.

The most unique feature of this book is its focus on the dynamics of difference and shame underlying what goes wrong—or what can go very right—with relationships. The dynamics of difference and shame have the power to set up the development of a *false self*. The false self defensively refuses to assert the *real self*. A dominant false self is a prescription for chronic *low self-esteem*, with a belief that the self is too impaired, weak or ineffective to merit esteem. This "essential phoniness" leads to a hollowness of life where blame of other or of life in general may ensue. Overcoming the power of these dynamics is the source of transforming unhealthy wounded relationships into healthy and healing real relationships.

Who Is Creating Real Relationships *For?*

Creating Real Relationships is for partners: married or unmarried, heterosexual, lesbian, or gay. It is for new lovers in the initial phases of a relationship. It is for people who have been together for many years and need to improve specific skills in their relationship. It is for those somewhere in the middle who find themselves unsatisfied with the realities of their relationship.

This book is for people who continue to be committed to each other and who still are willing to work toward a more satisfying life together. You will need the patience and persistence to keep working on a real relationship over time, because the skills and concepts required will not always result in instant gratification. It is more like a hard-work miracle. It won't happen by itself, or overnight—you and preferably your partner will have to work hard for it—but false, destructive relationships *can* be transformed into real ones that heal and nurture both partners, and in which love can thrive.

The new responses and behaviors you are about to try each require a number of weeks, sometimes months, to take hold. Significant change will require you to make several shifts in your response behaviors, and this will also take some time. You may try something new and it will seem like a disaster. It may not fit your style of being in the world or your particular needs. Taking risks means opening yourself up to possible failure. You will need to risk failure in order to reap fulfillment. If something doesn't work, try again or pick yourself up and move to the next skill.

Creating Real Relationships is *not* for partners who are *now* experiencing the threat of violence within their relationship. Physical threats or abuse requires specialized professional help, and it is recommended that you seek assistance at once. The breach of trust that battering causes to individuals goes beyond the scope of this book.

Creating Real Relationships is also *not* for people who are dealing with *active* drug or alcohol abuse. Substance abuse also requires specialized professional help, and it is recommended that you seek assistance at once.

However, *Creating Real Relationships* will be significantly helpful to people recovering from domestic violence and substance abuse, as well as to those in their families.

What Is the Self?

The *self* is the sum total of one's inner experience. The self is the individual personality structure. It has affective (feeling) and cognitive (thought) elements, which function at both a conscious (aware) and unconscious (unaware) level. The self attempts to evolve toward wholeness and maturity. However, it requires support in order to do so. If essential emotional needs are not adequately met or there is trauma, growth and development of the self will be impeded around the particular trauma or emotional-need deficit.

Basic Assumptions About Human Development

The skills and concepts in this book make certain basic assumptions about human development:

1. The development of the self proceeds in an orderly and rather predictable pattern. The rates of development may vary from individual to individual.
2. The development of the self passes through a series of hierarchically ordered and sequenced phases.

INTRODUCTION and SELF-ASSESSMENTS

3. These phases each contain developmental skills and dynamics that must be resolved if the individual is to proceed successfully to the next level of development. (The developmental skills and dynamics are included sequentially in the chapters of this book.)
4. The developmental skills and dynamics occur within the context of the individuals' early interpersonal relationships.
5. The developmental skills and dynamics also occur within the individuals' process of separation and individuation.

What Is a Real Relationship?

A *real relationship* supports, encourages, and nurtures both partners' real self. It is composed of two emotionally healthy partners who seriously and mutually consider each other's basic needs. Each partner is aware of his or her needs and is able to express these to the other freely. The couple has the skills to understand and accept these needs and to negotiate and resolve conflicts of needs as they arise. Specifically, both individuals in a real relationship have the capacity to:

1. <u>Experience a wide range of feelings deeply.</u> Accept a wide range of feelings in proportion to the situation, without fearing the expression of feelings. (However, not let guilt and disappointment run wild.) Don't block appropriate expression of feelings or erect barriers against them.
2. <u>Expect appropriate need satisfaction.</u> Expect that life can be mastered and good things can be achieved. Discover the physical and emotional conditions that contribute to pleasurable living, and act accordingly.

3. <u>Be assertive and self-activate.</u> Identify the things that make up their individuality. Be responsible for planning and taking action that will improve situations. Pursue their own goals autonomously without prodding from other people.
4. <u>Acknowledge self-esteem.</u> Have confidence in one's own judgment, ability, power, and decisions. Maintain respect for, or a favorable impression of, oneself. Know when a problem or crisis has been resolved, and recognize one's self-reliance. Maintain a sense of self-worth through healthy ways of thinking.
5. <u>Soothe painful feelings.</u> Don't wallow in misery, but find means to experience comfort and hope. Confront distortions in thinking that lead to extreme feelings. Know that pain is not necessarily deserved, but simply *is* at times and can lead one somewhere they would not have gone otherwise.
6. <u>Make and stick to commitments.</u> Make personal commitments to relationships and career goals. Persist in the face of obstacles, utilizing the support of others to assist them when needed.
7. <u>Express creativity.</u> Develop the ability to replace old, familiar patterns of living and problem solving with new, more successful ones. Devising ways to cope with loss or misfortune and improvise ways to achieve security. Find and express passions and interests.
8. <u>Experience intimacy.</u> Express the real self fully in a close relationship. Don't allow fear of abandonment to prevent intimacy from emerging at the beginning of a new relationship. Sustain intimacy through difficult times or when other goals must be pursued. Keeping healthy boundaries in relationships.

9. <u>Accommodate and enjoy being alone.</u> Be alone without feeling abandoned. Sense that the ability to find meaning in life comes from within, even if it ultimately involves others. When alone, enjoy being preoccupied with worthwhile pursuits. Don't confuse feeling alone with the loneliness and despair that leads to depression. When feeling despair, confront it rather than filling time with meaningless or ineffective activity.
10. <u>Find the unified real self that is you in the midst of all of your conflicting parts.</u> Recognize and sustain an awareness of the inner core of feelings, perceptions, values, and beliefs that persists and is the same as a person grows and develops, in good times and in bad times.

Relationships are more or less real. There are varying degrees of realness, and the degree of realness may fluctuate over time even within the same relationship. Couples who want a real relationship continually strive for the optimal in mutual respect, honesty, and emotional authenticity while at the same time seeking to resolve differences. A real relationship is a maturing relationship that accepts, encourages, and nurtures the growth and realness of the partners. A real relationship supports the movement from false self to real self. Look at the false self versus real self comparison table on the next page.

Real Self / False Self Criteria

False Self	Real Self
Extreme anxiety and/or no anxiety	Healthy level of anxiety
Extremely passive and/or rigidly aggressive	Assertive
Critical, judgmental, self-righteous, envious	Accepting and encourageing of self/others
Masked, camouflaged	Authentic, genuine
Distrusting and/or overly trusting	Healthy level of trust
Plans according to rigid schedules	Spontaneous while maintaining reasonable schedule
Withholding	Giving
Withdraws from communication	Communicative
Fearful, contracting	Expansive, loving
Always a responsible parent	Ability to be childlike
Pretense of invulnerability	Vulnerable when appropriate
Suspicious "What do they want from me?"	Accepting of people at face value
Desires isolation and shelter	Desires freedom and growth
Repeats old patterns	Can learn, adapt, and change
Denial of the unconscious	Open to the unconscious
"All or nothing" thinking	Balanced thinking
Split-off body, mind, emotions	Integration of body, mind, emotions

The movement from false self to real self is a process that takes time, but it can be significantly speeded up in the context and support of a real relationship. The goal of this book is to help develop this context and support.

INTRODUCTION and SELF-ASSESSMENTS 9

Working Individually or Together

Many of the chapters in *Creating Real Relationship* are designed for making one-sided changes in your relationship. These skill chapters will show you how to alter your patterns of interaction. This is of value because of the nature of relationship dynamics. When you change, your partner must change in response. If you take a new action or response, your partner will have to respond in kind. Even the simplest shift in the pattern can cause a major change in the dynamics.

Given human nature, your partner will more than likely resist your new actions or responses. Many people find change, even when it is good for them personally and/or for the relationship, a bit unnerving. This is when you need courage and persistence. If you keep trying and hanging in there with the new action or response, your partner can shift in a more effective direction as well.

Individual work can be quite effective, but working together as a partnership will be more efficient and satisfying. Both of you will be concentrating on the same objectives, and you will be able to encourage and complement each other with your efforts.

Assessing Your Emotional Needs

Take some time for each partner to fill out the Emotional Needs Assessment individually. Complete the following and determine on a scale between 1 to 10, with 10 being "completely" (fulfilled), 1 being "not at all" (deficit).

Emotional Needs Assessment

As a preschool-age child	
I felt admired	1 2 3 4 5 6 7 8 9 10
I felt loved	1 2 3 4 5 6 7 8 9 10
I felt protected	1 2 3 4 5 6 7 8 9 10
I felt safe	1 2 3 4 5 6 7 8 9 10
I felt trusting	1 2 3 4 5 6 7 8 9 10
As a school-age child	
I felt secure	1 2 3 4 5 6 7 8 9 10
I felt competent	1 2 3 4 5 6 7 8 9 10
I felt needed	1 2 3 4 5 6 7 8 9 10
I felt treated fairly	1 2 3 4 5 6 7 8 9 10
I felt valued	1 2 3 4 5 6 7 8 9 10
As an adolescent	
I feel appreciated	1 2 3 4 5 6 7 8 9 10
I feel confident	1 2 3 4 5 6 7 8 9 10
I feel fulfilled	1 2 3 4 5 6 7 8 9 10
I feel important	1 2 3 4 5 6 7 8 9 10
I feel independent	1 2 3 4 5 6 7 8 9 10
I feel optimistic	1 2 3 4 5 6 7 8 9 10
I feel productive	1 2 3 4 5 6 7 8 9 10
I feel recognized	1 2 3 4 5 6 7 8 9 10
I feel respected	1 2 3 4 5 6 7 8 9 10
I feel worthy	1 2 3 4 5 6 7 8 9 10

Record your respective Emotional Needs Assessment scores in the Partner's Emotional Needs Record Table on the next page.

Partner's Emotional Needs Record

EMOTIONAL NEEDS	PARTNER A	PARTNER B
I felt admired		
I felt loved		
I felt protected		
I felt safe		
I felt trusting		
I felt secure		
I felt competent		
I felt needed		
I felt treated fairly		
I felt valued		
I felt accepted		
I experienced privacy		
I felt supported		
I felt heard		
I felt understood		
I felt appreciated		
I felt confident		
I felt fulfilled		
I felt important		
I felt independent		
I felt optimistic		
I felt productive		
I felt recognized		
I felt respected		
I felt worthy		

Circle all scores below a 5. These are the emotional need deficits that will considerably affect your relationship.

Discuss them with your partner, because the emotional need deficits that each partner brings to the relationship will require attention. Let's now take an assessment of any problems you can identify in your relationship.

Assessing Your Relationship Problems

Each partner is to fill out the Relationship Problems Assessment. Complete the following and determine on a scale of 1 to 10 (1 = no problem, 10 = a major problem).

Relationship Problems

Arguing	1 2 3 4 5 6 7 8 9 10
Anger	1 2 3 4 5 6 7 8 9 10
Anxiety/panic	1 2 3 4 5 6 7 8 9 10
Conflicting needs in relationship	1 2 3 4 5 6 7 8 9 10
Depression, discouragement	1 2 3 4 5 6 7 8 9 10
Disenchantment	1 2 3 4 5 6 7 8 9 10
Emotional distance, low intimacy	1 2 3 4 5 6 7 8 9 10
False assumptions about partner	1 2 3 4 5 6 7 8 9 10
Feeling deprived	1 2 3 4 5 6 7 8 9 10
Feeling hurt	1 2 3 4 5 6 7 8 9 10
Feelings of inequity, unfairness	1 2 3 4 5 6 7 8 9 10
Guilt	1 2 3 4 5 6 7 8 9 10
Lack of time together	1 2 3 4 5 6 7 8 9 10
Misunderstanding	1 2 3 4 5 6 7 8 9 10
Name calling, blaming, threats	1 2 3 4 5 6 7 8 9 10
Negativity	1 2 3 4 5 6 7 8 9 10
Not feeling listened to	1 2 3 4 5 6 7 8 9 10
Problems with in-laws	1 2 3 4 5 6 7 8 9 10
Unexpressed feelings	1 2 3 4 5 6 7 8 9 10

INTRODUCTION and SELF-ASSESSMENTS

Record your relationship problems in the Table below placing scores above 5 in the appropriate box. If either partner has a problem above 5, it will be considered a relationship problem.

Partner's Relationship Problem Record

PROBLEM	PARTNER A	PARTNER B
Arguing		
Anger		
Anxiety/panic		
Conflicting needs from relationship		
Depression, discouragement		
Disenchantment		
Emotional distance, low intimacy		
False assumptions about partner		
Feeling deprived		
Feeling hurt		
Feelings of inequity, unfairness		
Guilt		
Lack of time together		
Misunderstanding		
Name calling, blaming, threats		
Negativity		
Not feeling listened to		
Problems with in-laws		
Unexpressed feelings		

Circle the Relationship Problems and discuss them with your partner. You may want to come back later to help determine the key skills for creating Real Relationships needed in Part Two of this book.

Getting Started Building Your Skills

Having completed the Assessments, you can determine which *skill* you want to work on first. If you can see that work on several skills will be needed, it is best to work on one at a time. You have a lot to cover in this book. You're going to have some fun, but you're also going to have to work pretty hard. You can learn several things:

1. New strategies and skills for being in a real relationship.
2. Healthy concepts that will enhance your self-esteem.
3. The role of shame in your life, and how to overcome it.

There will be some work to do, and you will begin practicing what you've learned in real situations. Most of your time will be spent learning new skills and then practicing them. So roll up your sleeves and let's get started.

Clarifying Expectations

Take a little time here at the beginning of your work to think about some of the things you're hoping to get out of this book. There are no right or wrong answers to this. Please try not to leave out anything, even if you think it might be unreasonable. If they're your ideas, they are of value.

It's natural to come to *Creating Real Relationships* feeling either hopeful or hopeless. Relationship issues develop over a long period of time, and you may have been disappointed for many years. Your problems are unlikely to disappear overnight. What you will do in later chapters is work to develop realistic and manageable short-term goals that may or may not be symptom-related. For example, you may have a goal of "feeling less anxious alone at home when Charlie has to work late." Or you might have a broader goal like "learning to control my temper and not snap at people—including Charlie and also my colleagues at work."

You may frequently find yourself setting unrealistic goals and standards, and then being hard on yourself when you cannot meet them quickly. For example, "blowing up at Cindy only if several attempts at rational discussion of the problem don't work" is a much more realistic goal than "never raising my voice to anyone again, no matter how much the other person provokes me." Also, "learning ways to feel less anxious and enjoy myself when Peter is away on a business trip" is more realistic than "always feeling totally relaxed no matter what is going on in my life." Certainly willingness to tackle ambitious goals is a positive, promising quality, but change and growth are *not* about "all or nothing." The reality of life reflects *some* change and *some* growth taking place over a period of *some* time. It is important to remind yourself frequently to be patient with yourself. You are doing something challenging that takes persistence and courage! The recovery process you are about to begin as you work with *Creating Real Relationships* will continue long after you finish this book.

Chapter 2

Overcoming the Power of Difference

What difference does it make to you what someone else becomes, or says, or does? You do not need to answer for others, only for yourself.

Thomas A Kempis

Fantasy and Disenchantment

The earliest stages of a relationship are filled with fantasy. It is a romantic, mostly unconscious image of two partners becoming as one, of merger in a love where there is no *difference*. The primitive fantasy also includes the belief that the new unit will provide fulfillment of all human needs. Before long the fantasy fades and the dream of an encircling unity without dispute or discomfort dissipates. The loss of the fantasy leads to disenchantment, which follows the discovery that partners have different, sometimes conflicting needs. Some disenchantment is predictable.

No matter how attached or bonded two partners may be, each will eventually require very divergent physical and emotional needs to be met. In fact, a symbiotic partnership may be headed for an even harder fall from the partners' fantasized expectations. (Partners are more or less symbiotic, or psychologically merged together. If there are very few boundaries between the partners, they are highly symbiotic—for example, when partners frequently finish each other's sentences. If partners have healthy boundaries that respect each other's difference and individuality, they are less symbiotic.)

The most compatible partners are not exempt from the loss of fantasy and will experience conflicts of needs. Discovery of this inevitable disenchantment ushers in a significant challenge to *any* relationship. How the partners deal with the disenchantment of difference will determine the destiny of the relationship. Some areas of potential partner difference include the following.

1.   Ethnic. If the partners come from different ethnic backgrounds, this can affect their value judgments of each other's behavior, especially if the ethnic differences are never openly discussed.

2.   Language. Communication problems are especially apparent if the two partners speak different languages, such as English and Spanish. However, even within the English language, different regional dialects use the same term with different meanings, and people have different vocabularies for expressing themselves depending on their socioeconomic and educational backgrounds.

3.   Gender. Though there are exceptions to every rule, it is more common for men to be avid football fans and women to prefer romantic movies. As a generalization, more men in our society are uncomfortable discussing feelings openly. This can cause differences in approach to solving relationship problems.

4.   Political. When partners have strong but divergent political opinions, this typically creates friction between them, unless they can agree to disagree.

5.   Values. Partners may have different values about many issues: religion, the importance of work, whether the house must always be kept clean, and so on.

6.   Parenting. Many couples disagree about parenting styles, such as leniency versus strictness of discipline.

7. _Spending._ If one partner is much thriftier than the other, there will be tension. Also, if the partners spend equal amounts of money but have very different opinions about what it should be spent on—entertainment and clothing versus home improvement, for example—there may be conflict over that also.

8. _Family._ Friction with one's in-laws is so common that it has become a cliché, though certainly this is not the case in all partnerships. Relating to a different kind of family from one's own can help a person grow.

9. _Education._ If a high-school drop-out enters a relationship with a college professor, there will be issues for them to resolve about education level. One classic fictional example of educational disparity is Sam and Diane on the TV series *Cheers*.

10. _Relationship skill level._ One partner may be well hidden behind a wall of defenses, finding it very difficult to discuss feelings or resolve relationship problems. The other partner may be more skillful at talking things out openly.

11. _Decision making._ Some people mull over decisions for a long time before deciding what to do; others act more impulsively.

12. _Physical._ Partners may have different levels of sex drive. One may love to be held, while the other enjoys intercourse far more. One partner may want large meals served with clockwork regularity while the other prefers to nibble and snack throughout the day.

13. _Psychological._ Partners may have different levels of dependency needs. For example, Denise may feel as though she needs Jim more than he needs her.

The "No Difference" Fantasy

We know that all individuals are different. However, as partners begin an intimate relationship, a fantasy that differences will disappear and something of a "twinship" will emerge frequently develops. As mentioned earlier, "falling in love" partly includes the denial of troublesome differences. The denial lasts only so long, and partners soon become vividly aware of their differences. When faced with this awareness, some partners believe that the other will change and that the difference will then no longer be a problem. Some partners adopt the attitude that the other partner's difference is wrong or bad. With this belief comes a rejection of and/or resentment of the other partner's difference. This in turn results in an invalidation of the other partner's real self, and a consequent reinforcement of the false self or retaliatory response, leading to a destructive relationship pattern. The emotional needs of both partners are destined to remain unmet, often a repeat of their early family life. Love has discovered its debris.

Creating a real relationship requires fully recognizing the ultimate truth that all people are different, with different emotional need deficits and different levels of relationship skills. Real love does not require psychological and skill-level sameness but affirms and values difference. In fact, acceptance of difference and uniqueness is an important aspect of maturity and character.

It is helpful to understand the significance of difference in terms of human development. Research with infants has shown that infants cannot distinguish themselves from their mothers during the earliest months of life. It is as if they are one and the same. The infant is hungry, and the mother intuitively senses this and feeds the child. Thus the earliest experience of love is highly devoid of difference. The baby grows and develops in this dependent environment until he or she is ready to begin to separate. The "terrible twos" usher in the word "No" as the child is saying, "I'm not you anymore, I'm me" (a unique self). The young child has begun the long process of separation and individuation, with goals of becoming a healthy and unique real self. Love's debris is fostered by the *distorted belief* that our partner should always think, feel, and behave (do things) the same way we do. It is vital to realize that others must be unique, and that we ourselves must be different in order to be healthy, maturing human beings. Then and only then will the debris begin melting away.

Difference is usually associated with the judgment of being good or bad. The categorizing or labeling of difference is often destructive to human relationships. For example, to say that a partner is emotional rather than intellectual can carry value judgment with it. Experience tells us that the world generally places a more positive value on intellectual expression than emotional expression. If Partner A tells Partner B, "You are being emotional," Partner B may interpret this message as "You are being less than acceptable." Thus it is heard as a negative, nonconstructive criticism regardless of the intention of the message sender. If, however, Partner A and Partner B understood difference as not only good but also vital, then the message of being "emotional" loses its sting and becomes an affirmation of uniqueness and acceptability. Difference moves from negative judgment to affirmation and esteem in the process of real relationships.

Attraction and Difference

Why are two partners attracted to each other? Is it physical, intellectual, emotional, biological, psychological, spiritual, or is it some combination of these? Human attraction can defy rationality. We are often surprised when certain persons partner up and become a couple.

Freud points the way for us to unravel this mystery. His notion that all loves are new editions of experiences with the earliest caretaker is relevant. New lovers have a psychic connection with the earliest lovers: parents and/or caretakers. The earliest experiences of attraction make a lasting imprint on the future of romantic love. Thus the love that has been lost will have a major impact on the love that is found, and we are often not aware of the imprinting effect of our earliest experience of relationship.

Both boys and girls normally experience the earliest love bond with their mothers. This earliest experience is usually not conscious; we are unable to recall more than a brief image of our first 12 to 18 months of life. Yet in those early months, significant love and attraction are experienced.

When the toddler begins to individuate during the "terrible twos," the dawning of separation/individuation does not begin without a preceding internal psychic process. There have been an increasing number of moments during the first two years of life when the child has experienced the absence of immediate gratification of his or her needs. The mother or other caretaker has not always been attuned to the child's needs; the needs of the child and the needs of the caretaker have been experienced as different. By the time they begin separation/individuation, all children have uniquely experienced difference within the context of their first relationship. If a transforming bond accompanies the experience of difference in the first relationship, the separation/individuation process proceeds in a healthy way. A transforming bond is an emotional and physical connection, as well as a communicative process, that fosters a sense of trust and respect.

Emotional Need Deficits

The very young child has a need to receive from his or her primary caretaker(s) an *attunement* of both physical and emotional needs. The infant requires a bonding with the primary caretaker(s) that includes a sense of knowing and gratification of what the child needs and experiences. This type of bonding is called attunement. If enough attunement is experienced, the child moves ahead along the path of healthy development. However, if *not* enough attunement is experienced, woundedness occurs, and the child feels prematurely different or excluded. The woundedness becomes an emotional need deficit within the character of the child. The child no longer feels merged with the powerful, loved, and protective (mother/caretaker), and as a result of this growing awareness experiences anxiety, rage, a sense of helplessness, and intense ambivalence. To the extent that particular individuals have had difficulty negotiating such an early developmental process, the experience of difference reawakens many of these early, negative emotions. The desire to eliminate differences may simply be a preference for what is less stressful, more comfortable, and more familiar.

If this emotional need deficit is not worked through in childhood or adolescence, it is carried through to adulthood and into adult relationships. This is a similar psychological dynamic to shame, which is discussed further in Chapter 3. The feeling of exclusion or difference is too unpleasant, so the child develops psychological defenses to protect against further woundedness. The fantasy of no difference is also developing at this time.

Projective Identification

An adult child of an alcoholic (ACOA) walks into a crowded room of strangers and is immediately attracted to a person across the room who is later discovered to be an alcoholic. How does this powerful attraction occur? The answer lies partly in the unconscious mental process known as projective identification.

Two of the most useful psychoanalytic contributions are the notions that human beings have the capacity to perform complex communication on an unconscious level, and the unconscious mechanism of projective identification. Projective identification was first formulated by Melanie

Klein and has been extensively written about by both Kleinians and non-Kleinians. Without plunging into the complexities and nuances of both the intrapsychic and interpersonal aspects of projective identification, seekers of real relationships should have some understanding of this significant relational process.

For the purposes of *Creating Real Relationships*, projective identification involves taking an aspect (thought, feeling, impulse) within the self and projecting it out onto the other person. An integral element of this psychic process, known as "splitting," involves keeping the self good. For example, Kyle tells Brett that she looks depressed, when he himself actually feels down in the dumps. Kyle projects an aspect of his mental functioning (thoughts, feelings, impulses) onto Brett without being aware of what is really happening. This unconscious mental process allows Kyle to feel both "good" and identified with Brett. Brett responds by stating that she feels just fine and is not aware of any depressed feelings. Brett has tested reality for Kyle, who now has the opportunity to learn something more about his real self by becoming aware of the projection.

A similar process known as "introjective identification" refers to the unconscious introjection (taking in) of an aspect of another person's mental functioning (thoughts, feelings, and impulses) and identifying with it. For example, Partner A says to Partner B, "I feel depressed," when she has unconsciously noticed that Partner B looks down in the dumps.

These unconscious identification processes are a significant combination, which play out unknown to either partner, creating either a powerful bond or a sense of difference between them. It becomes a powerful bond when the aspect of the self projected out to the other or introjected from the other is acceptable (good) to the partner. It becomes a powerful difference when the aspect of the self projected or introjected is unacceptable (bad). For example, imagine a woman saying to her lover, "Oh, sweety, you're so irresistibly cute and cuddly!" because that's how she wants *him* to perceive *her*. But he's disgusted because he wants to be thought of as John Wayne.

Another example of a powerful difference dynamic is an ex-smoker who has strong feelings of contempt toward a partner who lights up a cigarette. The unacceptable or rejected aspect of the ex-smoker partner is projected onto the partner who acts out the impulse to light up. The felt difference of an ex-smoker and a smoker can be filled with strong feelings. If it is not worked through by talking about all the thoughts, feelings and impulses involved—those the two partners are aware of and those they may be unaware of—the difference can become destructive to the real relationship.

Complementarity

One of the hopes of real relationships comes from the interpersonal dynamic of *complementarity*. Complementarity is a relationship process in which each partner's missing qualities or deficits find wholeness through the contribution of the other's different personality traits. Complementarity provides the promise of mutual completeness through relationship. The principle of complementarity assumes that even the healthiest human beings have deemed some aspects of their real selves unacceptable. To grow up and mature requires that a child be told "no," "you can't do that," or "you are not acceptable for that." Experiences of unacceptability and shame are inevitable. Without these experiences children would be forever dependent on their caretakers and not become healthy, unique, mature individuals. How these necessary experiences are mentally worked through determine the cohesiveness and wholeness of the self. Essentially, life includes emotional need deficits. We cannot escape at least some woundedness.

When two people each search for the lost half of their self and find it in each other, complementarity is at work. Complementarity involves the possibility of both partners working out their emotional need deficits rather than rewounding their earlier scars. It is with good reason that partners sometimes call each other their other or better half. Through the discovery of difference in real relationships, partners also find the aspects of their self that require healing—and then are healed partly by each other, partly by themselves.

Complementarity allows for reality testing of your real self and your partner. From the initial attraction, you unconsciously began to merge the image of your partner with your primary caretaker(s). Then you began to project the unacceptable aspects of your self out to your partner, obscuring both the images of your partner and your self. However, the dynamic of complementarity enables you to gradually let go of your disenchantment and begin to see the truth that will set you free.

Here is an example of how complementarity might work in a relationship:

a. John's parents are cold and strict with him during his childhood and youth. He is discouraged from showing outbursts of temper or emotion of any kind. John learns to hide his feelings. He studies hard and becomes a successful accountant.

b. John meets Alice, a singer, and is charmed by her warmth and spontaneity. He unconsciously senses in her some of the qualities he wishes his mother had had. Alice, in turn, has led a rather chaotic, disorganized life and welcomes John's stability.

c. John projects onto Alice the emotional temperament for which his mother used to scold him. He sometimes gets annoyed with Alice—for exactly the qualities that drew him to her in the first place. She sometimes finds him

exacting and dull because he is not more like her. During this stage, projective identification is distorting both partners' views of each other and of their true selves.
d. However, as they both learn to respect and cherish each other's differences, they also learn to see and heal their own emotional need deficits from the past. John needs to relax and become more expressive and spontaneous. Alice needs to plan her time better and be more responsible about money.

Complementarity provides partners seeking a real relationship with a hidden purpose. Rather than simply focusing just on a facade of thoughts, feelings, and needs, partners learn to identify their emotional need deficits and the childhood issues that caused them. When complementarity is functioning creatively within a relationship, that relationship takes on more meaning, and partners have a greater sense of control and satisfaction. The relationship isn't just a goal in itself, but a means for self-discovery, healing, and personal growth.

The skills that are required for a real relationship are the same needed to work through the emotional deficits of the past. The path toward real relationships and healing the wounded self requires a great deal of support, nurture, and encouragement. Let's turn our attention to one resource for help.

Spirituality

There is truth to the paradox that accepting difference opens us up to realize a oneness that underlies our relationships. A spirituality of difference finds a oneness in difference and diversity. Although we are all different and unique, we are also very much the same, needing the basic physical and emotional elements of life for our aliveness. We seek a partner who has enough sameness to be compatible, but it is the differences of the other that cause the mystical "chemical attraction." The following are some helpful spiritual aspects for the journey of real relationships:

Spiritual aspect of humanity. Humanity is to be celebrated as a miraculous part of creation. Everyone belongs to the human race, without exceptions. There are no tests to take, no duties to perform, no possible way to be eliminated. All people are human. No amount of shame can take away our innate grace.

Spiritual aspect of humility. Humility is the full knowledge of our limitations. All human beings are equal, with no person better or worse than another. Humility allows for difference by acknowledging that we are limited and different. Each of us has the right and responsibility to decide how to live our lives. Every person is good enough to contribute some value to the world.

Spiritual aspect of gratitude. Gratitude is the realization of the goodness you possess. It means letting go of the fear and anxiety of deprivation long enough to experience the joy of what you authentically are and do have. Gratitude transcends the angst of life and is an antidote for greed and envy.

Spiritual aspect of grace. Grace is the profound realization that you are acceptable, you belong, and you are good enough just the way you are. All partners need to be assured that they are human, normal, and competent. These reasonable human needs are especially not met in *shaming relationships*. Shaming relationships are formed when two shamed partners come together as a couple. The spiritual aspect of grace will be particularly significant for shamed partners.

Spiritual aspect of realness. *Realness* involves being in touch with what you think, feel, and need. There are many forces that can pull you away from experientially knowing these things at any given moment. For various reasons you may have learned to focus on what others might think, feel, or need in order to please them. However, this doesn't work in the long run because it is ultimately inauthentic. Realness is a spiritual path of finding truth within your self and being free from the fears associated with the consequences of being real.

<u>Spiritual aspect of meditation.</u> Meditation comes in many forms, numerous methods, and various techniques. It can look like prayer or silence, and it can be practiced formally and informally. Meditation is an invitation to notice when you reach your personal human limits or when your life is out of balance. The practice of meditation is helpful in finding clarity, moving toward flexibility and openness, and discovering and developing your real self.

Chapter 3

Overcoming the Power of Shame

While his mother talks to a neighbor outside the house, a two-year-old child explores the outdoors. He finds a special place nearby where he digs happily in the soft soil. He feels proud of his accomplishment. "Look at me," he wants to tell the world. "Look at what I can do. I am good." "Just look at this mess!" says his mother with scorn. "Look at you. You are filthy dirty! Your clothes are ruined. I am disappointed in you. You ought to be ashamed of yourself!" The child experiences himself as very small. He drops his head and stares at the ground. He sees his dirty hands and clothes and begins to feel dirty inside. He believes there must be something very bad about him, something so bad he can never really be clean. He fears his mother's disdain. He sees himself as defective.

Shame as an Inevitable Human Experience

Most of us have felt shame because, as mentioned earlier, it is perhaps an inevitable human experience. We have all suffered feelings of incompetence, inadequacy, and inferiority. We have known a sense of failure or defect and have been scorned or unacceptable to another. *Shame* is among the most painful of human affects (feelings). If we listened to it all the time, we might be driven to take desperate action or just give up in despair. This shame often seems too painful to endure, which helps us to understand why it often goes underground to our unconscious. We may defend against our shame so well that we are literally unaware of its existence.

Healthy and Unhealthy Shame

Shame and guilt can sometimes be confused. Guilt is when you have *done* something wrong. Shame is when you *are* something wrong. For example, a child might feel guilt if she broke her mother's vase and hid the pieces, but she might feel shame if her mother then told her she was a clumsy, no-good sneak who would never amount to anything.

Shame can be healthy or unhealthy. Healthy shame is normal and temporary, and it provides specific messages for you that maintain a healthy balance for your thoughts and behavior. For example, if you feel shame about showing up late to work, that motivates you to show up on time after that. Most people can stand up to normal, temporary shame. That kind of shame certainly hurts, but it will eventually disappear.

Unhealthy shame, by contrast, is excessive and distorted. Feelings like "I don't deserve a better life than this because I'm just a rotten person" have nothing to do with reality and have a very damaging effect on your thoughts and behavior. Partners with unhealthy shame have been shamed more than normal, by prolonged, repeated, or perhaps chronic events. Excessively shamed partners feel as though their shame can never go away, whether it is conscious or unconscious. This is the shame that shows up as low self-esteem and all its attending difficulties in relationships.

Excessive shame begins for the infant with his first significant relationship. This is usually the mother-child relationship because the mother is most often involved as the primary care-taking adult. For example, the little boy at the beginning of this chapter internalized the judgment of his mother. Her words came precisely at the developmental stage when a child is just beginning to assert some independence. As stated earlier, two years old is the time when children first begin to become a unique self, to say "No," "I'm not you...I'm me." If the mother has some problem with her child's attempt toward autonomy, the child is ripe for experiencing excessive shame. The shaming continues to develop in the family of origin, and is encouraged by an overly shame-focused culture.

Shame and Relationships

Relationships inevitably cause emotional pain, regardless of how loving or caring the partners might be. Partners can say things that unintentionally cause hurtful feelings to each other. They do not wake up in the morning and think about what they can say that will be hurtful. Partners experience pain in relationships as a result of hearing a message, which is interpreted either consciously or unconsciously as shame. Each partner's personality structure is made up of various defenses designed to ward off this shame.

These defenses—such as denial, withdrawal, and anger—can do a couple of things. They help avoid or cope with uncomfortable or painful emotions. However, they also can undermine the relationship. Real relationships, in an effort to support the partners' emotional openness, encourage their vulnerability of thoughts and feelings. This openness itself can arouse hurtful shame feelings for both partners. When Partner A says something that makes Partner B feel bad and unworthy, Partner B wants to stop the hurt. The usual response is to defend against the pain. How Partner B protects is mostly a result of his or her individual style and what was learned in the early family interactions. Partner B might get angry and counterattack, or do something to distract Partner A from the issue, or turn off emotionally and withdraw. Partner B will use whichever defense he or she has learned from early family experience as good protection from painful feelings.

There is nothing inherently bad about protecting oneself from pain. In fact, defenses against shame or other uncomfortable feelings are a healthy dynamic. The difficulty lies in the destruction that can result in the relationship. Defenses can result in distance because they tend to undermine trust. Denial, avoidance, emotional withdrawal, or angry attacks—while providing a temporary armor of safety—become destructive barriers to intimacy.

Defenses Against Feeling Shame

Anna Freud first described how feelings such as shame are so intolerable to the ego that it develops certain mechanisms to push them away from consciousness. The partner who represses shame may not even be aware that he or she is defending against feelings of shame. The partner may not even recognize shame as the problem. Defenses against shame may help a person deal with feelings of self-hatred and pain, but in the long run they do not heal shame. No one can learn to benefit from shame by ignoring it. Defenses against shame are only survival strategies; excessively shamed individuals must stop relying on their defenses before they can learn and experience that they are valuable individuals who are worthy of love and respect. The way out of shame is to come out of hiding.

Thoughts excessively shamed partners defend against include:
a. I am defective (damaged, broken, a mistake, flawed)
b. I am dirty (ugly, unclean, impure, filth, disgusting)
c. I am incompetent (not good enough, inept, ineffectual)

d. I am useless (worthless)
e. I am unwanted (unloved, unappreciated, uncherished)
f. I deserve to be abandoned (forgotten, unloved, left out)
g. I am weak (impotent, feeble)
h. I am bad (awful, dreadful, evil, despicable)
i. I am nothing (worthless, invisible, unnoticed, empty)

Denial

The first kind of defense against shame is denial. Those who are in denial simply stay unaware of their shame. They deceive themselves into believing they have no shame, when in fact they would experience great shame if they were fully aware of what was happening internally. They badly want to believe they are completely acceptable to themselves and to others, so they blind themselves to whatever would bring them shame.

People who are excessively shamed often live in a world of appearances. They will do anything to protect their image as good people, even if that means ignoring reality. For example, many alcoholics deny their drinking problem. They would feel tremendous shame if they admitted they couldn't control their alcohol use. They believe something must be wrong with anyone who is powerless over a mere bottle. They cannot understand how someone could be both an alcoholic and a good person at the same time. They believe: *An alcoholic is a worthless bum. I'm not that way. I'd hate myself if I were a drunk. I can't be an alcoholic.* Their fear of overwhelming shame is so strong that they are blinded to the evidence of addiction.

Denial of shame is not exclusive to alcoholics. After all, shame threatens the core identity of a person. Whatever could bring shame to someone can be defended with denial. We defend what we dare not see. Living in denial, however, takes its toll on a person. Slips of anger control can cause lots of problems. It is essential in recovery to face reality even when it is excruciatingly painful. But you can only do that when you learn that you can survive your shame. The way out of shame is to come out of hiding.

Withdrawal

Another survival strategy against shame is withdrawal. People withdraw when they have endured so much shame that personal contact with others is too painful to handle. Flight is a normal reaction to situations when people feel exposed and vulnerable, and withdrawal is a common reaction to shame. Remember that the initial physical reaction to shame is to break eye contact and look down or aside. People who are shamed more or less say to their companions: *Right now I feel so bad about myself that I cannot look you in the eye. I can't stay close to you because that will only increase my shame.* Already feeling "naked" before the world, people who are excessively shamed certainly don't want another person to stare at them. They believe, at least temporarily, that everyone can see their soul, see that they are inadequate and bad.

Partners who are excessively shamed also withdraw in other ways. Perhaps they evade uncomfortable topics of conversation or stay emotionally unavailable to others. Some people practice the art of low visibility. They are always there but not visible. One example is when very talented people stay behind the scenes because they are so afraid of exposure that they let others take credit for their accomplishments.

A partner who is excessively shamed can become trapped in withdrawal from others. He or she may do anything to keep others distant, as if they had already shamed him or her. Direct, meaningful, or intimate connections to others are very threatening to people who do not feel good about themselves. "Not feeling good about yourself" is code for shame. Keeping others distant is a protection from the humiliation of being judged or rejected.

Perfectionism

Another defense against shame is perfectionism. Perfectionists dread making mistakes because they think mistakes prove something is fundamentally wrong with them as a person. If they fail at something, they believe they are a total failure. The perfectionist who is defending against shame seems only to recognize two states of being: perfect or shameful (all or nothing). Such people fight desperately against being human because they equate accepting humanness with being a failure. But we are all simply human—people who must do the best we can given our limitations in strength, intelligence, creativity, and wisdom. It is not shameful to be less than perfect when none of us have a choice in the matter.

Perfectionists may not be particularly arrogant. They are not really trying to play God when they try to be faultless. They are simply trying to hold shame at bay a little longer. They feel a tremendous pressure to perform, to demonstrate to the world and to themselves that they are adequate. Constantly aware of the possibility of shame, they are convinced that others are watching for imperfections and will judge them to be worthless when those flaws are discovered.

Excessively shamed individuals sometimes have perfectionistic traits even though, deep down, they are not really perfectionists. The house must be spotless before company arrives; a project never gets finished because it has several flaws; a person, trying to do a job faultlessly, stays at work or school long after others have gone home. It seems that such excessively shamed people must take *great* pride in their accomplishments in one realm of life and *none* in other realms. Whatever the manifestation of the excessive shame, the goal is to avoid humiliation. Their failures seem permanent to them—no matter what they do, old failures cannot be redeemed. Yet successes seem temporary—they could vanish in an instant. Shame is never far away.

As you can see, perfectionists are in a no-win situation. No matter how competent they are, regardless of how well they perform, despite all their successes, perfectionists never feel more than one step ahead of shame. They can delay humiliation for a while, perhaps by working harder or longer than anyone else. But they cannot feel comfortable for very long either, because they do not know how to accept themselves as a good, but limited, human being.

Arrogance

Ordinarily, shamed persons believe they are smaller or lower than others. The words "beneath contempt" describe how shame feels. But what about shamed individuals who convince themselves that the opposite is true—that they really stand head and shoulders above everybody else? Such people have discovered arrogance.

There are two ways of displaying arrogance: grandiosity and contempt. Grandiose people inflate their sense of self-worth so that they believe they are better than others. Contemptuous people put others down to make them seem smaller than themselves.

Imagine two people as two equally inflated balloons. Now imagine pumping up one of the balloons until it is so full of hot air that it is ready to burst. That is grandiosity. The grandiose person hides her shame from herself and others by filling up with pretentiousness and false pride. She needs to feel superior to cover up her underlying sense of shame. She deludes herself into thinking that she is naturally the best of all living creatures.

Now imagine someone who goes around deflating balloons. That is contempt. The contemptuous person will find a way to deflate other people, making them feel weak, incompetent, and shameful. This type of person defends against shame by giving it away to someone else. Such people feel better about themselves only when they reduce others to nothing.

Some excessively shamed persons practice grandiosity; others practice contempt. Many use both forms of arrogance to protect themselves against their inner sense of shame. Arrogant people place themselves on a pedestal where nobody can see their shame, not even themselves. The price they pay is not being connected to others. Someone on a pedestal cannot be warmed by the beauty of intimacy. Arrogant people have set themselves apart from all those who would or could love them. True, arrogant people avoid feeling worse than others do by exchanging feelings of inferiority for feelings of superiority. But they fail to touch or heal the center of their pain—their shame.

Creating a Self-Centered Universe

Most people learn when they are young that they cannot be the center of the universe. Some people do not want to accept this idea. Perhaps they never learned to gracefully relinquish being the center of attention when they were children. This situation begins to become shame deficiency, shamelessness. Such people want to be placed on a pedestal where they can be adored. They are egotistical to the point of having no room to care about others. This is different from arrogance, where the person consciously behaves in a way to compensate for a felt inadequacy. The shameless person has a distorted belief system that leads to shame deficiency.

Rage

What happens when a person who is deeply shamed cannot withdraw from a threatening situation? Rage, another survival strategy against shame, is a likely response.

The rageful person is shouting a warning: *Don't get any closer! You are getting too near my shame, and I won't let anyone see that part of me. Stay away or I will attack.* A rageful person is desperate to keep others far enough away so they cannot destroy him.

People are most apt to fly into a rage when they are surprised by a sudden attack on their identity. For example, Paul might offhandedly tell his buddy Jake that his clothes are too cheap and loud for Jake to get a date with a certain woman. Paul might be joking, not intending to hurt his friend. But Jake is hurt and lashes back: "What do you mean, I couldn't get a date with her? I sure look a whole lot better than you do—at least I don't walk with a limp like you." This shamed individual can only think to defend himself by attacking the other person.

Rage works. It drives people away and therefore protects the person from revealing his shame. Sometimes it works too well. People start to avoid rageful people who are oversensitive to supposed insults. "I would like to be Jake's friend," the person might say, "but whenever we start to get close, he finds something to get mad about. Then he attacks me for no reason."

Rageful people's strategy to defend against overwhelming shame is very debilitating to their self-esteem. Such people will probably feel all the more defective when others become too scared to reach out to them. Rage breaks the connection between people and so increases the shamed person's shame. Chronically rageful people become trapped in a lonely world of their own making.

Anyone might respond with rage occasionally, especially if they are suddenly and unexpectedly embarrassed. But persons with excessive shame may express their anger more often. Their regular bouts of rage cover up deeper shame. Their attacks on others direct attention away from their sense of inadequacy.

Chronic Shame is Relentless and Devastating

Chronic shame—unlike the temporary, healthy shame discussed earlier—can have several kinds of devastating effects on people and their relationships.

Shaming Yourself Excessively

All people occasionally shame themselves; in other words, they are self-critical. After all, shame is part of life, and moderate shame can help you mature emotionally. Excessively shamed persons, however, are so full of shame that they regularly attack themselves with this weapon. These individuals can truly be called excessively shamed because they respond to the world through the lens of their shame. They suffer from such an excess of this feeling that they seem to take their shame lens wherever they go.

Excessively shamed people expect others to confirm their badness by putting them down with criticism and contempt. Even a positive response from others is often irrelevant to the excessively shamed person. The crucial point here is that such people are constantly telling themselves that they are no good. They expect others to confirm their shamefulness mainly because *they* are convinced that others will view them in the same way they see themselves. Nor will such people quickly change their self-perception in the face of praise and acceptance. They will stubbornly cling to the idea that there is something fundamentally wrong with them. They are ashamed to exist.

Excessively shamed people have taken their shame into the very center of their being. Their shame comes automatically to them because it is a deeply engrained habit of thinking. Such people's core of self-hatred and disgust gets activated time after time. They end up attacking themselves mercilessly. "I feel totally empty—worthless and useless. My life has lost its meaning. I set goals for myself that nobody could meet, and then I despair about my failures. No matter what I do, I can never be good enough to please myself. The funny thing is that I put all this pressure on myself. Nobody else is unhappy with me. Why can't I live with myself when everybody else can?"

People lose energy when they give themselves these messages. Some give themselves so many of these messages that they consistently withdraw from healthy relationships or healthy activities. They retreat or prepare to withdraw whenever they believe they are once again doing something wrong.

Shame that cannot be removed gradually turns into self-hatred. It is as if there is a black hole in the person's soul into which his or her goodness is lost forever, leaving a residue of disgust and contempt. Thinking only about the badness inside, such people miss the beauty of their own humanity. They see ugliness instead of beauty, shame instead of grace, and weakness instead of strength. Self-hatred is not subtle or sophisticated. The messages we are referring to are basic and crude. They may include profanity and deprecation.

Shame and the Fear of Abandonment

The fear of abandonment is central in people who have excessive shame. Abandonment seems quite possible to people who believe that they are basically worthless and unlovable. Why would anyone stay with them when there are so many better persons in the world? Excessive shame prevents people from believing that they are good enough to be cherished.

"I Will Be Whatever You Want Me to Be"

Fearing abandonment, people who are shamed may try to please others by becoming whoever others want them to be. Their reasoning is clear: *I'm certain that they would be revolted if they saw the real me. I must please them by being a person they would be proud of. That's the only way they will keep me.* People like this spend most of their time reacting to others. Their self-worth depends on the praise and criticism they receive from outside themselves.

Self-Sabotage

Self-sabotage is a way to be self-destructive. Julie sabotages herself when she "forgets" to enroll on time in a program that would advance her career; Michael consciously refuses to take medication as prescribed that would ease his depression. These people undermine their chances for success and happiness because they think they do not deserve anything positive. Internalized shame demands failure. Self-sabotaging people choose continuing shame over success at least in part because their rage at themselves allows no room for competence or achievement.

Self-Abuse

Self-abuse is an active result of shame. Here, people who are deeply shamed seek out ways to damage themselves. Certainly some shame-connected addictive behaviors are nothing less than slow suicide—the alcoholic who continues to drink despite liver damage. Other forms of self-abuse include calling oneself names like "stupid" and knowingly entering into damaging relationships with shamers.

Self-Neglect

Self-neglect occurs when people who are excessively shamed ignore their own needs by. For example, failing to see a physician despite a severe illness, refusing to eat balanced meals, and neglecting their appearance. Each of these actions demonstrates passive self-hatred.

The Tendency to Humiliate Others

Shame is a threat to a person's basic sense of well-being. Excessively shamed people feel small, weak, vulnerable, and exposed. They may rage against themselves because they feel unacceptable. They might also find this self-hatred unendurable. Sometimes, in order to survive, people who are excessively shamed transfer their hatred onto others, treating them with the disdain and contempt they often experienced themselves. Unfortunately, excessively shamed people become parents who attack and humiliate those over whom they have the most power—their family. The family victims receive the parents' criticism, verbal and sometimes physical assaults, never allowing for any success or happiness. The more a shamed parent loves the children, the more that parent needs to reduce the children to nothing, so that the children cannot do the same to the parent. Shamed parents shame their children to avoid their own shame.

Compulsive / Addictive Behaviors

Shame and addiction are natural partners. The more chronically and excessively shamed people are, the more likely they will be attracted to anything that promises relief from internal pain and emptiness. They believe the answer must lie outside themselves in the "magic" of alcohol, other drugs, mystical religious movements, consumer goods, sex, food, work, the latest therapy or fad, and so on. Shamed people are trying to fill the void that has been at least partially created by excessive shame. They simply cannot stand being in pain or feeling empty inside.

Note here that shame alone does not cause addiction, any more than an addiction causes shame. Each contributes to the other. The person who is excessively shamed is a high-risk candidate to become addicted, and the addicted person frequently becomes more and more shamed as the addiction worsens.

Have Patience: Healing Shame Is a Process

Lack of patience is often a hallmark quality of shame. The healing of shame is a process, not an event. It takes time and requires that you give yourself a break by not being too hard on yourself.

Stage 1: Understand and Accept Your Shame

Shame is about a person's identity as a human being. Since the wounding from shame is frequently deep and long-lasting, it will take time to feel better. The recovery from shame is a gradual process, not a one-time event. You might feel terrible one day, better the next, and maybe awful again on the third day.

Impatience is a problem as you deal with shame. You naturally want relief from that feeling as quickly as possible. Furthermore, just reading and thinking about shame can temporarily seem to intensify the problem. Above all, you need your shame to go away so that you can feel your right to exist in the world.

A real danger lies in shaming yourself even more by rushing off too quickly to "fix" your shame. Remember that you cannot force liking or respecting yourself. Self-care has to build gradually. Shame can be replaced with dignity and pride, but only slowly. If you try to heal your shame too rapidly, you may only add another "failure" to your list.

At first there may be more bad days than good. But after a few months or perhaps a year or longer, you may discover that you respect and appreciate yourself much more than when you first began to heal your shame. The gift of love for yourself is the payoff for dealing with shame and self-hatred.

Become Fully Aware of Your Shame

Shame is not easy to face. After all, who wants to explore exactly how one holds oneself in contempt? Many people dread the terrible feelings of self-hatred that lie deep inside them and are embarrassed to admit that they have such thoughts. Healing your shame will take courage. You will have to examine your shame even though your natural impulse is to hide from it.

How do you improve your awareness of shame? Completion of this workbook and following the exercises and homework assignments is the best start. More specifically, notice the messages your body gives you. Clues that shame is present include blushing, looking down, and sudden loss of energy—rapid deflation of the self. You should also listen carefully to your thoughts, especially the automatic insults you give yourself. You can also detect shame in your actions. If you isolate yourself from others or withdraw verbally or emotionally, you may be feeling shame. Perhaps you feel paralyzed (unable either to approach or to retreat from a situation because of overwhelming self-consciousness), perfectionistic, or criticized by people around you. Still another way to improve your awareness of shame is to explore your spiritual connections and disconnection. How do you find meaning in your life? When do you feel less than fully human?

Shame episodes can be small or great. If you have committed yourself to becoming fully aware of your shame, you will need to notice the smaller shame events, especially those repeated regularly. Shame can become a habit when smaller shame events go unchallenged.

Explore Your Defenses Against Shame

Earlier it has been mentioned that excessively shamed partners often develop survival strategies that lessen their awareness of shame. These defenses minimize the immediate pain at the cost of ignoring reality. Think about the common defenses against shame that you may be using.

a. <u>Denial:</u> denying the parts of life that bring you shame, forcing your real problems out of your consciousness.
b. <u>Perfectionism:</u> trying to hold off shame by striving to never make a mistake and do everything perfectly.
c. <u>Arrogance:</u> acting superior to everybody or insisting that others are full of defects. (Arrogance has two parts: grandiosity and contempt.)
d. <u>Creating a self-centered universe:</u> focusing on one's own needs and insisting that others pay attention to them as well, even at their own expense.
e. <u>Rage:</u> driving others away so that they cannot see your defects. This is most likely to occur if you believe others are deliberately trying to humiliate you.

The goal here is to understand how you protect yourself from painful shame feelings and thoughts, not just to get rid of your defenses. Eventually, you will be able to make choices about how to defend yourself. For example, if you habitually withdraw from others when you start to feel shame (or when you fear that you could start to feel shame), you should not feel obligated to stick around and work through shame issues in public. You have the right to stay or leave, depending on what you can handle at the time.

Explore the Sources of Your Shame

It is valuable to sort through the various sources of your shame because each leads to different healing strategies. For example, if your main problems with shame come from living with an arrogant and demeaning partner, your healing will require a different approach than if your feelings of shame come primarily from childhood. Many people discover that their shame is related to several sources.

Explore Your Shaming Relationships

Shame is corrosive. It eats away at a person's dignity, pride, and self-respect. Unfortunately, many people become embroiled in shaming relationships that feature daily episodes of humiliation. These relationships may be one-sided—only one member shames the other. One-way shame often occurs when one person enjoys a power advantage over the other. Two-way shaming relationships happen when both parties vigorously and regularly shame each other. These people engage in shaming contests in which the goal is to degrade the other more.

Shaming relationships are dehumanizing. *All of us deserve to be treated with respect, no matter what the nature of our association with another person is. Others deserve our respect.* Any relationship that centers on shame dishonors its participants.

Although, as stated earlier, excessive shame usually begins quite early in life, you may now be involved in relationships that increase your burden of shame. Few people are strong enough to stand up to continuous shame attacks by important people in their lives. How can you feel really good when told repeatedly that you are incompetent, worthless, ugly, or stupid? How can you feel healthy pride while listening to messages that you will never be good enough to satisfy your family, friends, or employer? The formula is simple: the more you are shamed by others, the more shamed you will feel. Every person is entitled to a life free from excessive shame. The more you have suffered shame, the more you expect it.

It is easy to have strong feelings when thinking about shaming relationships. You may find yourself reacting strongly, especially if you are now in such a relationship. Keep a few thoughts in mind:

1. Someone who regularly shames you may be unaware that he or she is doing so. Not all shame episodes are deliberate.
2. You may be both a victim and a victimizer. This means that persons who are shamed by others often repeatedly spread shame as well.
3. *Shaming relationships can be changed.* If both parties in a relationship realize that there is too much shame, they may be able to alter their behavior.

Accept Your Shame as Part of the Human Condition

The understanding phase of resolving shame ends when you accept yourself as a human being who occasionally feels shamed. Your shame will not go away by your fearing, hating, and fighting it. In fact, it could even grow stronger if you fight it. A person who despises his shame forgets that he detests himself in the process. *You must accept your shame before you can change it.* That is a reality. Shame cannot simply be wished away because it is painful. Nor can it be willed away through being tough. It is far better to befriend your shame than it is to treat it with dread or hatred. All of us feel ashamed of ourselves occasionally. Try to make peace with that shame if possible, because it is really another part of you. We must respect every part of ourselves, including our shame, to discover our love for ourselves.

Stage 2: Take Positive Action

Shame is a messenger, telling you that there is something wrong in your life that you must change. You need to pay attention to that message and then take action that will help you live a better and more meaningful life.

Get Help–You Don't Have to Do This Alone

Isolation is a common reaction to feelings of shame. The more deeply you are shamed, the more you will hide your thoughts, feelings, and actions from others. People who are shamed keep vast areas of their lives a secret because they believe that others would scorn them if they knew who they really were. Unfortunately, shame prospers in secrecy. By concealing your identity if you are deeply shamed, you only convince yourself that you are fundamentally defective.

However, much of shame develops and grows through our relationships with others. That shame can best be addressed when we come out of isolation and communicate with others. Damage from shame begins to heal when that shame is exposed to others in a safe environment.

Not every person can be trusted with your shame. Above all, a trustworthy person is one who will not add to your shame or humiliation when he or she is given private information. Because you may have difficulty talking about yourself, you need to make a commitment to reach out to others at the very times when you feel least acceptable. You need to move toward others even if you are terrified of rejection. At the same time, you need to protect yourself by seeking nonshaming persons with whom to share, so that your acts of courage will not be met with damaging attacks. (*Note:* Nobody can respond to you every time with care and compassion.)

Challenge the Shame

Each source of shame must be challenged a little differently. For example, a depressed woman might need to tell herself all five of the following statements at some time during her recovery from excessive shame:

a. That's my depression telling me I'm no good. I can't stop that from happening now, but I know it's not true.
b. My parents told me I was worthless and I believed them. Now I'm an adult and I can refuse to accept those messages any longer.
c. My partner criticizes me ten times a day. It's time for me to tell her clearly that I won't keep living that way. I'm worth more than that.
d. I'm tired of hating myself. For one thing, I'm going to make a commitment not to call myself terrible names anymore. I need to treat myself with respect.

Heal the Shame from Your Family of Origin

You carry around with you an invisible set of parents who live inside your head. These parental images might repeatedly remind you that you are defective. Furthermore, these "old" parental figures may remain in place even if your parents are no longer alive or have significantly changed and no longer shame you in the same way they once did. The most common kinds of behavior that produce shame from the family of origin are:

1. Psychological abuse, or deficiency messages such as that you are not good, you are not good enough, you are not lovable, you do not belong, or you shouldn't exist.
2. Threats of abandonment, betrayal, neglect, disinterest.
3. Physical or sexual abuse.
4. Keeping secrets that would be appropriate to reveal.
5. Parental perfectionism.

The Difference Between Exploring the Past and Getting Stuck in It

The goal in exploring your past is to discover how events have damaged you, so that you can change your current thoughts, feelings, and actions. While you are "researching" your shame, you will feel pain. But it is important that you work through the hurt rather than get stuck in it. You must bring your head as well as you heart with you, maintaining at least some emotional neutrality to balance your suffering.

Try not to exaggerate events as you explore the past. Probably no parent *always* shamed his or her children. See if you can recall some times when your parents or other family members praised you, helped you, and clearly appreciated you. Remember that you are dealing with a parent, not a monster. Ultimately your shame must be kept in perspective to lessen the risk of getting caught up in the past.
The more deeply you have been shamed, the harder it will be to unglue yourself from previous disappointments, traumas, and abandonment. As you explore the cave of your past, let your friend or a therapist be your rope, and let your commitment to a healthy future be your flashlight.

Decode Deficiency Messages Received from Your Family

The most important deficiency messages are those that affected you the most deeply. These statements might feel correct when you say them to yourself. *Yes, my father always called me a dummy. But he was right. I am stupid.* The messages are painful, and they seem fixed forever.

It is helpful if you can remember specific incidents from your childhood that involved these deficiency messages. Perhaps you were called clumsy or lazy by a parent as you did chores. Perhaps a parent would no longer touch you after you reached puberty. The incidents may be powerful or small, repeated regularly or occasionally.

Grieve Your Life Losses Resulting from These Messages

Deficiency messages like those listed above, and other shaming behaviors, profoundly affect the developing child. A child who receives deficiency messages will have many needs that go unmet. The recovering adult must grieve these unmet needs.

All children want to hear that they are loved, that they belong, they are good enough just the way they are, and that they are totally acceptable to their family. They need to be assured that they are human, normal, and competent. These reasonable needs are not met in habitually shaming families.

Some losses can never be replaced. No amount of praise or respect in adulthood can compensate for the lack of praise or respect received as a child. That is why mourning is a necessary part of healing shame. You must mourn the parts of you that seemed to die in the face of rejection.

Grieving helps you realize that shame attacks the spirit. When we face losses resulting from shame, we feel a penetrating sorrow that can fill us with pain. But this grief can relieve shame when it is experienced fully. It helps us to put away the past, with its lost hopes, so we can find a new path in the future.

Challenge Old Deficiency Messages

The best thing that can happen to you if you came from a shaming family is to grow up. No matter how terrible your situation, you are not as helpless and dependent as you were as a child. As an adult you can challenge the bad messages you received as a child. You may have had little choice about accepting these messages before, but you can replace them now with much healthier ones.

Remember that these messages originated outside of you. They may have been sitting inside your head for years, but they did not begin there. You can sort through the messages you received in childhood and consciously decide to throw some out. When you challenge the shaming messages you received as a child, you can take the following steps:

1. First, identify each specific shaming message.
2. Second, identify the person or people who sent each message.
3. Third, challenge the idea that the message must be true.
4. Fourth, consider the message and accept or reject it.
5. Fifth, substitute new, positive, nonshaming messages for the old, shaming ones.

Challenge Your Behavior

The hard work described in the preceding section pays off when you change your actions to live a less shame-focused and healthier life. This new behavior may begin with acquaintances, friends, and more intimate relationships. Eventually, though, you will have to alter your behavior with your family of origin or with others who substitute for your family (such as authority figures).

Shame that originated in your family heals best when you change your interactions with your family or family substitutes. Parents do not have a right to shame their children just because they are parents. "Dad," you might say, "you have called me an airhead for years. I'm not an airhead and I've never been one. Please don't use that term again." These confrontations will not be easy. They will probably be met with angry and defensive tactics, especially if the shame attack is intentional. The best challenges to a shaming family are those that are presented calmly and clearly. They may also have to be repeated regularly, because shaming families tend to return to old, shaming behaviors out of habit. Some family members or their substitutes *can* change, and some will do so fairly quickly once they learn that you insist on fair treatment. Others may change reluctantly or not at all. You will have to decide how much time and energy you will devote to the task of changing your family interactions.

Return "Borrowed" Shame

Shame is contagious in shaming families. It can easily pass from one family member to another, finally affecting everyone. Sometimes one or more people will gather the shame that belonged to another family member. This shame is transferred from its rightful owner to more vulnerable people.

This shame is called "borrowed." The goal is to focus on the possibility of returning it to its original owner. The idea is that, at one time, a person was "loaned" shame against his or her will. This shame originated from the behavior or attitudes of another, usually more powerful, family member. Now this shame must be returned before the healing person can embrace a nonshaming view of himself or herself. All that is meant by returning borrowed shame is letting others take responsibility for their own behavior or feelings.

Borrowed shame may be given to a specific family member either intentionally or unintentionally. Often it happens when the family cannot stand the humiliation of the real problem. For example, it is far easier to blame and shame a child than to cope with a father's drunkenness. *You ought to be ashamed of yourself, young woman! If you got better grades and caused less grief, your father wouldn't get so upset and have to drink.*

Certain children may be blamed the most for family troubles. But others in the family may also borrow shame. Other children are held up as examples and will collect shame and guilt when they fail to keep everybody happy and everything perfect. Parents can and do feel borrowed shame as well, for the actions of a child.

The key to healing shame received from borrowed shame is in recognizing when you are feeling shame about something that has nothing to do with you or your actions but results from another family member's behavior. If you are returning borrowed shame, you may tell yourself:

Long ago I took on some shame that didn't belong to me. I thought it was mine at the time. So did the rest of my family. But now I know that I did nothing at the time that was wrong. I'm not guilty, and I have nothing to feel ashamed about.

If the family members involved are still alive, you can directly communicate your resolve to no longer accept their shame. The main goal here, however, is to come to this realization within yourself so that the old borrowed shame no longer damages your spirit. If you do speak with family members, the point is *not* to punish them by insisting that they now should feel humiliated.

So far you've had an overview of difference and shame: why people can feel these feelings excessively, how they defend against them for their own protection, and how these defenses can cause distance in relationships. You've seen how to work at overcoming shame within yourself. Now let's move on to Part Two and learn the skills necessary for creating real relationships. Remember, as stated earlier, these are the same skills that will help you heal your old wounds of shame.

PART TWO

KEY SKILLS FOR CREATING REAL RELATIONSHIPS

Chapter 4

Developing Assertiveness Skills

Every noble work is at first impossible.
Thomas Carlyle

Three Basic Types of Communication and How They Affect Relationships

One of the joys of living is the satisfaction of by getting some of your physical, emotional, and spiritual needs met in a real relationship. Partners' ability to assertively communicate their needs to each other requires healthy beliefs and communication skills. Let's begin by looking at three types of communication.

Assertive Communication

Assertive communication involves clearly stating your needs—how you feel and what you want—without violating the rights of your partner. The underlying assumption in assertive communication is: "You and I have differences, and we are mutually responsible for expressing ourselves respectfully to each other." The significant hallmarks of assertive communication include getting some of what you need without alienating your partner, active participation in making important decisions, the emotional and spiritual satisfaction of respectfully exchanging thoughts and feelings, and healthy self-esteem.

Partners who communicate assertively speak in a relaxed, clear tone of voice. They make good eye contact and have unanxious posture. Here is an example of an assertive exchange between partners:

Partner A: I wonder if we might discuss our holiday plans? I would like to take a break from traveling to your parents this year. I've been really tired lately and I could use a breather around the holidays. We could stay home and just take it easy.

Partner B: Well, I would really like to visit my parents this year.

Partner A: We did go there last year and we've visited with them a couple of times already this year.

Partner B: I realize that, but it's not really the holiday to me unless I'm with my parents.

Partner A: How important is it really to visit with them at the holidays this year?

Partner B: On a 10-point scale, it's a 10 for me. How important is it to you to stay home?

Partner A: Well, I guess about 7 or 8. OK. What if we go this year for just a few days and make some alternative plans to come home and spend time together and get some rest after our visit?

Partner B: All right, that sounds reasonable!

Aggressive Communication

In aggressive communication, needs, feelings, and wants are honestly stated, but at the expense of the other partner's feelings. Aggressive communicators are usually loud and direct. They tend to use sarcasm, rhetorical questions, threats, negative labels, profanity, you-messages with absolutes ("You never clean up the living room anymore"), glaring, and literal finger pointing as communication weapons.

Here is an example of an aggressive partner speaking:

Aggressive Partner: You are such a slob, as far as you're concerned I guess we might as well live in a junk yard! I don't care if it takes you all weekend to get the house clean. If it is not straightened up by Sunday afternoon, I'm going on vacation without you.

The underlying message in aggressive communication is: "I'm superior and right, and you're inferior and wrong." The advantage of aggressive behavior is that people often give aggressors what they want just to get rid of conflict. The major disadvantages are that aggressiveness can cause partners to retaliate or get even in some way. Aggression tends to create resentful and adversarial partners.

Passive Communication

In passive communication, needs, feelings, and wants are withheld altogether or expressed only partially or indirectly. The passive communicator tends to speak softly. Eye contact and posture are often poor, conveying a message of submission. Here's an example of a passive partner's response:

Passive Partner: (under her breath) I don't get enough out of this relationship to have to take this kind of abuse! *(then out loud, after a big sigh, with faint sarcasm)* I'll get it done right away, dear.

The Principles of Assertive Communication

Assertive communication is based on the assumption that partners are each the best judge of their own thoughts, feelings, needs, and behavior. They are better informed than anyone else is about their family background and current circumstances that shape them into unique human beings. Partners are each best qualified to express their position on important issues. Since partners are unique, there are many times when they will disagree. Rather than submit to or overpower the other, partners each have the right to choose to express their position and try to negotiate the differences.

Passive partners tend to believe that their thoughts, feelings, beliefs, and needs are not as important or valid as those of the other partner. As children, they learned to seek affirmation from their family authorities, and to doubt their own perception and judgment. As adults, they tend to submit to others' needs. When conflict arises between what they need and what a partner may expect of them, they feel guilty, wrong, anxious, or stupid if they say no to their partner.

Partners who lean toward the aggressive type of communication often have an inflated sense of their own importance and feel entitled to whatever they want without considering the needs of others. Often found under this pretense of self-importance is a deprived early self. As children, aggressive partners were often abused by their parents/authorities, and they later developed an aggressive type of communication in lieu of passive victimization. Some aggressive partners took away from their early childhood experiences the belief that they are entitled to overpower others. Intolerance to difference learned in childhood can also result in an aggressive communication style. Partners who are aggressive need to consider the needs and feelings of others as well as their own.

Assertive Rights

Children have no choice about the beliefs they were taught. However, adults have the option of choosing whether or not they are going to hold onto the beliefs that

DEVELOPING ASSERTIVENESS SKILLS 63

discourage assertive behavior. The following are examples of distorted beliefs that discourage assertive behavior and the corresponding helpful assertive rights.

Table 1: Distorted Beliefs / Assertive Rights

Distorted Beliefs	Assertive Rights
It is shameful to make mistakes. **	You have a right to make mistakes**
It's selfish to put your needs before others.	You have the right to put yourself first sometimes.
If you can't convince someone that your feelings are reasonable, then your feelings must be wrong.	You have a right to be the final judge of your feelings and accept them as legitimate.
You should respect the views of others, especially if they are in a position of authority...Keep differences of opinion to yourself.	You have a right to express your own opinions and beliefs.
You should always try to be logical and consistent.	You have a right to change your mind.
You should be flexible and adjust.	You have a right to question what you don't like and to protest unfair treatment.
You should never interrupt people. Asking questions reveals your stupidity.	You have a right to interrupt or to ask for clarification.
Things could get even worse; don't rock the boat.	You have a right to negotiate for change.
You shouldn't take up others' valuable time with your problems.	You have a right to ask for help or emotional support.
People don't want to hear about your pain, so keep it to yourself.	You have a right to feel and express pain you feel.
When someone takes time to give you advice, you should take it seriously.	You have a right to ignore advice of others.

Distorted Beliefs	Assertive Rights
Knowing that you have something special or have done something well is its own reward. People don't like showoffs. Success is secretly disliked and envied. Be modest when complimented.	You have a right to receive formal recognition for your special qualities and talents and for your work and achievements
You should always try to accommodate others. If you don't they won't be there when you need them.	You have a right to say "no."
Don't be antisocial. People will think that you don't like them if you say that you would rather be alone than with them.	You have a right to be alone, even if others request your company.
You should always have a good reason for what you feel or do.	You have a right not to justify yourself to others.
When someone is in trouble, you should give help.	You have the right not to take responsibility for somebody else's problem.
You should be sensitive to the needs and wishes of others, even when they are unable to tell you what they want.	You have a right not to have to anticipate the needs and wishes of others.
It's always a good policy to stay on people's good side.	You have a right not to worry about the goodwill of others.
It's not nice to put people off. If questioned, give an answer.	You have the right to choose not to respond to a question or situation.
You should be able to answer all questions about a field of knowledge with which you are familiar.	You have the right to say "I don't know" or "I don't understand."

***It is shameful to make mistakes.* This distorted belief requires some further discussion. How many times as a child did you hear, "Shame on you!" when you made a mistake? The implication was that if you did something incorrectly, it was bad, and you were bad for doing it. Your value as a person depended on your actions, so it became very important to do well and please others in order to feel good about yourself. When self-worth becomes closely tied to performance, then you feel shame whenever you make a mistake. You would merely feel regret if you viewed your mistake as a slip in performance. Regret is a useful emotion in that it motivates you to minimize and correct your mistakes. Shame can serve the same function, but it can also deteriorate your self-esteem and contribute to impulse behavior. Partners who are prone to shame believe that only perfection (100 percent) is good enough.

Partners who believe that it's shameful to make a mistake are likely to avoid taking risks, even if it means forfeiting their rights. Others may use fear and shame of making mistakes to take advantage. For example, when a shame-prone partner asks for help with the banking, his or her partner responds with "I remember that you forgot to pay all those bills last month. That's not the behavior of someone who deserves a favor." And the shame-prone partner backs down because he or she agrees with the criticism. The association of mistakes with shame inhibits healthy assertive behavior.

Now let's consider the assertive right to make errors. Just as a toddler learns to walk by falling down many times, we learn from our mistakes. Anything worth doing right is worth doing wrong at first—and even once we've learned how to do it well most of the time, we won't always do it perfectly. (Even Major League baseball players sometimes drop the ball!) Errors have the added benefit of keeping us humble. Only God is perfect; to err is human. The assertive right to make errors does not free us from the consequences of our errors; we are still responsible for our actions. However, it does free us from the shame of equating our actions with our self-worth. When we simply acknowledge our errors and do not feel ashamed of them, we become resistant to manipulation. For example, when your partner points out that you failed to pay some bills last month, and uses this as the reason for not doing you a favor, you don't give up in shame. You respond with, "You're right, I did make that one error, for which I'm sorry. Now let's talk about what I've done right for our relationship lately." A healthy belief in the freedom to make errors promotes learning, assuming appropriate risks, and being creative. It encourages assertive behavior.

You may still believe that some of your negative beliefs about assertiveness are correct, or you may be having trouble with some of your assertive rights. While your belief about assertiveness may have been true for you as a child, ask yourself whether the same situation must exist for you as an adult. As an adult you have more power and many more choices for coping with these situations.

Confront Your Fears of Being Assertive

It is quite helpful to ask yourself the following questions:
1. If I'm assertive in this situation with my partner, what is the worst thing that could happen?
2. What beliefs do I have that would lend probability to this happening?
3. Is there any evidence to support this belief?
4. What evidence is there to refute this belief?
5. What would be a more realistic negative outcome of my being assertive in this situation?
6. How might I respond to or cope with this more realistic negative outcome?
7. What is the best thing that could happen?
8. What is going to happen if I continue to do what I have been doing?
9. Is it worth it to me to be assertive in this situation?

Here is an example of this process at work:
- If I tell George I'd rather not spend this year's vacation at his parents' house again because I don't particularly enjoy his mother's company, he'll get furious and divorce me.
- He loves his mother more than he loves me.
- George calls his mother every week; he does try to be a good son.
- Now and then he's told me that his mother gets on his nerves too. And he does love me. He told me so just last night and gave me a big hug.
- He might be annoyed with me for a little while, and we might have a heated discussion about where to spend our vacation without spending much money.
- I could be prepared with some suggestions for alternatives that might appeal to him: a couple of nights at a bed and breakfast, a camping trip, a visit to friends.
- We could end up having our best vacation ever, somewhere new and exciting.
- We'll keep spending all our vacations at his parents' house. Nothing will change unless I take the initiative to break our old routine.
- Yes.

Criticism as Manipulation

Many partners have difficulty dealing with criticism because they experience it as personal rejection. As a child, you probably faced criticism from a rather powerless position. When you made a mistake, your parents and other authority figures passed judgment on you: "Jeanne, you shouldn't have broken your sister's toy. Bad girl." You had expressed some aggression; therefore you were bad. Eventually you learned to feel ashamed whenever you were criticized. This is a rather destructive form of manipulation used to teach children to conform. However, it can have a lasting impact on a child's ability to be assertive. Less damaging ways of instructing children in how to behave involve reinforcing appropriate behavior and ignoring unwanted behavior, pointing out what is wrong with the behavior and suggesting a more desirable alternative behavior, and the modeling of appropriate behavior.

Assertive Approaches for Dealing with Criticism

Partners may have developed special coping mechanisms to minimize the pain of criticism that have followed them into adulthood, such as blowing up, recalling the faults of the critic, or acting as if they didn't hear the criticism yet still feeling miserable inside. These extremes of aggressive and passive approaches to dealing with criticism can damage real relationships as well as self-esteem. The following are fourteen assertive approaches for dealing with criticism that will help you simultaneously keep your relationship and self-esteem intact. The approaches include acknowledgment, sorting, agreement in part, agreement in principle, agreement in probability, clarification, the content-to-process shift, the broken-record approach, slowing it down, stating your position, active listening, taking turns expressing and listening, making a relationship compromise, and saying no and sharing negative feelings.

Acknowledgment

When your partner offers constructive criticism, you can use this feedback to improve yourself and the relationship. When you have made an error, having your partner point it out to you in a logical way can be helpful in preventing future mistakes. Whenever you receive criticism with which you agree, whether it is constructive or simply a reminder, acknowledge that your partner is right. For example, "Yes, I did put on one purple and one green sock this morning. Thank you for pointing it out." You are not required to give excuses or apologize for your behavior. When you were a child, you may have been asked questions such as "Why did you knock over the trash?" or "Why were you forty-five minutes late?" You were expected to give reasonable answers, and you learned to come up with reasonable excuses. As an adult, you may choose to give an explanation for your behavior, but it is not necessary. You can decide whether you really want to, or whether you're just responding out of habit.

Sorting

A nonconstructive criticism with which you disagree may require the use of an assertive approach known as sorting. The nonconstructive criticism of a partner usually contains a grain of truth with a spin of his or her imagination in order to put you down. For example, "When can we get going? You're always late. Sometimes I wonder how you keep your job." Partners who employ nonconstructive criticism tend toward name calling and you-messages. When they are in a critical emotional state they may bring up old history or use absolutes such as "always," "never," and "everyone." If you try to reason with them, you may only give them more ammunition for their case. They may not be interested in listening to you at this point, even when they ask you a question. Their present fragile ego state may require them to be right and to win their point. As you're tempted to justify yourself or retaliate in kind to the nonconstructive criticism, remind yourself that you will only feed a senseless argument, which you cannot possibly win. If you are still unconvinced, think back to a similar situation when you have tried to reason or get even with you partner. Why continue to waste your time doing something so unpleasant and unproductive? Try some alternative ways to sort out the criticism. Sorting involves distinguishing the piece of truth from the spin of nonconstructive criticism. Here are three ways to do this.

Agreement in Part

This method of sorting involves finding some piece of the manipulative critic's statement that you think is true, and agreeing with it. Reframe your partner's statement in a way that does not jeopardize your integrity. Delete the absolutes and leave out the nonconstructive part of the message. In response to the example above, you might simply say, "You're right, I am late sometimes." Your partner may try to get you to admit to more than you wish. As long as you persist in staying with some part of your partner's statement to agree with, he or she will probably give up on trying to prove the spin.

Agreement in Principle

The next method of sorting involves agreeing with your partner in principle. This utilizes simple logic: if X, then Y. "If I am always as late as you say, then I would have truly lost my job long ago." Here is another example of an agreement in principle response. Your partner might say, "You did a lousy job cleaning the dishes. They still have grease on them. You're the laziest person I've ever met! You're not going to make it at your new job if they catch you working like this!" You might respond with, "You're right, I wouldn't be a very good dish washer at a restaurant if I left grease all over the dishes."

Agreement in Probability

The third method of sorting that you can use with a partner who employs nonconstructive criticism is called agreement in probability. Choose something within your partner's critical statement with which you could probably agree. You can remind yourself that the odds of this one piece of the statement being accurate are minuscule as you reply, "You're probably right that I'm frequently late." Reframe your partner's wording slightly so that you maintain your integrity.

Clarification

At times when you are unsure about your partner's intent, clarification may be in order. Whether your partner is trying to help you, however clumsily, or putting you down intentionally, makes a difference. Is your partner actually trying to hurt you under the guise of being helpful? Are your partner's comments actually hiding unspoken beliefs, feelings, and desires? To clarify the intent of your partner's statements, you may want to clarify by listening carefully—a major feat, especially if you have a history of being criticized. Here is an example of clarification.

Partner: Late again, I see. One of these days you'll arrive at work only to find that everyone else has gone home for the day.
You: What is it about my being late that bothers you?
Partner: I work hard all day with a ton of pressure on me. You have a much more stress-free job, and you still don't get dinner on the table on time.
You: What is it about my easier schedule that *really* troubles you so much?
Partner: I haven't had a vacation in over a year, and I work overtime every weekend. You take it easy all week and make almost as much money as I do. It's just not fair.
You: I didn't know you felt so strongly about this lack of fairness stuff!
Partner: Well, now that I talk about it out loud, I guess I don't really believe that life is fair. I guess I made my own choices for working so hard and you've made decisions along the way so that you don't have to.

In this situation, clarification was helpful in placing responsibility for the dissatisfaction where it belonged: with your partner. Sometimes your partner will not have so much insight or tendency toward clarification. When you've assured yourself that the criticism is nonconstructive or manipulative, shift from clarification to sorting. If you agree with the criticism, acknowledge it. Be careful when you clarify that you do not either verbally or nonverbally give the message "So what's the problem now?" (suggesting that you view your partner as a complainer). When used appropriately, clarification can turn a partner who employs judgmental criticism into an assertive individual who directly expresses his or her thoughts, feelings, and needs while also honoring yours.

The Content-to-Process Shift

If a conversation with your partner gets stuck because of conflict of needs or strong feelings, you can shift the focus of the discussion from the presenting topic to an analysis of what is happening between the two of you. Try not to be further diverted by explaining why your partner has brought up old issues. Simply state that the conversation is off the point. Rather than argue about this you can simply say, "I'm just stating my opinion" and then you can quickly return to the original topic.

For example, you are asking your partner to talk to you more, and he or she responds: "You feel like I'm emotionally abandoning you? I can recall on our summer vacation you only spoke to me about three times." Instead of getting into an involved discussion about the issues of the vacation, you can say: "We're getting away from the problem at hand," or "Maybe you are angry with something I said."

The Broken-Record Approach

The good news is that you have the assertive right to express what you think, feel, and need. The bad news is that partners may misunderstand each other's assertive need to stand up for their rights. The broken-record approach is one of several assertiveness skills that will help you deal more effectively with your partner and others.

As with a broken record, the key to this approach is repetition. You will need to recall your assertive rights if you are giving in to your partner's needs too easily. Occasionally you will encounter a situation where your partner will not take no for an answer. When you want to set a limit and your partner is having difficulty getting your message, you may need to take a stand and stick with it.

This technique is also effective in communicating to your partner what you need when his or her interests are preventing him or her from seeing yours. For example, you may ask your partner to do the dishes after you have spent two hours preparing dinner.

Here are the five steps of the broken-record approach:
1. Decide exactly what you need or don't want. Assess your thoughts about the situation, your feelings, and your assertive rights.
2. Create a brief, specific, easy-to-understand statement about what you need. A single sentence is best. Don't offer excuses or explanations. It is most effective to say "I don't want to...," or "I'm not comfortable with...." In wording your brief sentence, eliminate any loopholes that your partner might use to further his or her position.
3. Employ assertive body language to support your sentence: good posture, direct eye contact, and a calm and self-assured voice.
4. Firmly repeat your brief sentence, as many times as necessary for your partner to get your message and to realize that you won't change your mind. He or she will

probably invent a number of excuses or simply say no. Eventually even the most aggressive person will run out of no's and excuses, if you are persistent and logical in your approach. Change your brief sentence only if your partner finds a serious loophole in it.
5. You may acknowledge your partner's opinions, feelings, or wants before returning to your broken record. But do not feel obligated to answer questions. Be careful not to be distracted from your goal.

Slowing It Down

The urgency to fix a problem too quickly usually is the result of anxiety. You don't need to respond immediately to every problem or have an instant answer when your partner raises an issue. Slowing it down helps in a number of ways. It gives you a chance to better understand what is really being said by allowing your partner to express all his or her thoughts and feelings. Some momentary delay also gives you a chance to experience your thoughts, feelings, and needs regarding the issue. Finally, slowing it down helps prevent a knee-jerk response that you may later regret. Lack of urgency will allow both you and your partner a chance to discover a more satisfying resolution.

Stating Your Position

You can use a statement of your position in order to express your thoughts, feelings, and needs regarding an issue. The situation may be a little one, such as which movie to see with your partner, or a big one, such as explaining to your partner why you want to change your career. In either case, you need to articulate your position clearly and completely in order to avoid misunderstandings. There are four parts to a good statement of your position:

1. Your understanding of the situation
2. Your feelings regarding the situation
3. Your needs regarding the situation
4. An incentive to encourage your partner to cooperate

Your understanding of the situation is a definition of the problem. This part is necessary for focusing the discussion. It is your chance to state your beliefs regarding the problem situation. Nonjudgmental, noninflammatory, objective language will be most effective. For example: "We need to make a decision about what we want to see at the movies tonight. I know you really like action films, but we've seen one the last three times we've gone out. We could use some variety!"

The second part, expressing your feelings regarding the situation, gives your partner a sense of how important the problem is to you. Try not to mix up an opinion for a feeling here. An example of a feeling is, "I dislike action films!" Once they are stated, your feelings play a significant role in helping you get what you need, especially when your opinion is drastically different from your partner's. Your partner may be able to relate to your feelings regarding an issue, even when he or she totally disagrees with your opinion. When you express your feelings, the problem becomes less of a competition. Expressing your feelings can make a mutual compromise more possible.

The third part, expression of your needs, is most effectively stated in a few simple sentences. State your wishes and needs clearly. It is not appropriate to expect your partner to read your mind even if you have a childlike desire to be given what you want without having to ask for it. Be specific about what you need. Ask your partner to change behavior, not attitudes. For example, "I would really like to go to a romantic comedy tonight."

The fourth part of a statement of your position is to encourage your partner's cooperation. Let your partner know how he or she will benefit by cooperating with you: "We'll both be more interesting and well-rounded," or "I'll be more enthusiastic about going out on Saturday night." If your partner is very resistant, incentives may not work. In this situation you may need to state the negative consequences for failure to cooperate. When describing negative consequences, do not make threats such as this: "If we don't go to a romantic comedy, I'm going to make your life miserable." This will only bring out defensiveness and hostility. State how you will take care of yourself if your needs are not accommodated: "I'll have to invite a friend to go see the romantic comedy."

Sharing with your partner your thoughts, feelings, and needs in a statement of your position increases the possibility that the message you want to send will be the message your partner receives. It is important that the statement of your position does not blame or use destructive language. Otherwise your partner is likely to become defensive, tune out what you are saying, counterattack, or withdraw. Your position should be described specifically and objectively without negative judgments. By using I-messages as opposed to you-messages, you own your thoughts, feelings, and needs.

A statement of your position is difficult for your partner to blow off. Your statement may be new to your partner however, and they may become momentarily silent. Don't let this deter you. After some time you may want to say, "I'd like to hear some feedback on what you heard me saying." Then remain silent and wait for a response from your partner.

Active Listening

Listening actively focuses your attention on your partner so that you can accurately hear his or her thoughts, feelings, and needs. Active listening involves three steps.

First, prepare yourself by becoming aware of your own thoughts, feelings, and needs. Second, listen by giving your full attention to your partner. Listen to his or her way of viewing the situation, feelings, and needs. If you are not clear about any of these three elements, ask your partner for more information. For example, "I'm not clear about how you see the problem. Would you be a little more specific about it?" or "How do you feel about this?" Thirdly, acknowledge your partner's comments by using reflective listening. For example, "If I hear you right, you're saying that you don't want to go to another action film tonight because you prefer romantic comedies and you're feeling like we need more balance in our life. Is that what you're telling me?"

Taking Turns Expressing and Listening

When you are involved in a conflict of needs with your partner, the two of you can take turns expressing and listening. Simply stating clearly what each of you thinks, feels, and needs may produce resolution to many problems. It can clear up misunderstandings or create unexpected solutions to problems. These opportunities may present spontaneously, but more often you will need to be intentional about arranging a mutually convenient time and place to discuss the situation. Here is an example:

Partner A: I'd like to discuss the toilet seat with you. Is this a good time?

Partner B: How about after the TV show? It should be over in half an hour.

Partner A: (after the TV show is over) The toilet seat may seem like a silly thing to you, but it's been bugging me ever since we got married. I believe that the correct position for the toilet seat is down. I'm tired of having to put the seat down when I have to use it, or landing on the cold porcelain when I go to the bathroom at night. I get angry with you for leaving the seat up.

Partner B: Well, I can understand your preference for having the seat down, and I can hear your irritation. To be honest with you, I prefer the seat up. I'd rather not have to put the toilet seat down after I use it.

Partner A: I feel the same way, and I'm usually in more of a hurry than you are!

Partner B: I think you're being self-centered. It's just as important for me to have the seat up as it is for you to have it down. Your need seems unfair to me. I'd rather that you leave the seat in the up position for me.

Partner A: No way, although I do see what you mean. I feel stuck. Even though I may be asking for something that you think is unfair, I still want my way on this.

Partner B: Look, if you'd be willing to put the seat up after you use it next month, I'll put it down after I use it this month.

Partner A: Ok, but let's talk again after a few months to see if we want to try working out another solution. Maybe we need to think about adding another bathroom!

Partner B: All right then. Let's try the cheaper way first!

Making a Relationship Compromise

When two partners' needs are in direct conflict, a negotiation that will completely satisfy both partners is difficult to achieve. Instead, you can look for a relationship compromise that you can both live with, at least for a while. Here are some examples of relationship compromises:

- Some of what I want and some of what you want.
- If you'll do *a* for me, I'll do *b* for you.
- My way when I do it, your way when you do it.
- My way this time, your way next time.

Although a relationship compromise can spontaneously result from your discussion, you will sometimes need a brainstorming session to come up with one. Brainstorming a relationship compromise involves four steps:

1. List all the alternative solutions you can think of. Let your creative juices flow while generating as many solutions to the problem as possible. Don't judge any of the options at this stage of brainstorming. Just list as many possible solutions as you can, even if some are silly.
2. Eliminate the solutions that are not mutually acceptable.
3. Identify a relationship compromise that you can both live with.
4. Agree to evaluate the relationship compromise after a period of time. If you aren't both adequately satisfied at this time, you can renegotiate. If your compromise seems to have sufficiently resolved the conflict, celebrate your effectiveness as a couple.

An alternative method of reaching a relationship compromise involves having your partner counter your proposal. If you find the counterproposal to be unacceptable, make sure that you understand your partner's thoughts, feelings, and needs regarding the problem situation, and think of yet another proposal. Continue until a mutually acceptable proposal is found. A helpful question to ask if you're both having difficulty arriving at a relationship compromise is, "What do you need from me to feel OK about doing this my way?" The answer to this question may serve as the basis for a workable compromise.

Saying No and Sharing Negative Feelings

Learning how to say no and share negative feelings is an important real relationship skill. Assertiveness problems often originate in families where there were inadequate boundaries and limits. Your parents likely tended to be overly permissive, overly strict, or inconsistent. In addition, it may have been unacceptable to express your negative feelings appropriately. As a result, you were never exposed to the skills necessary to maintain appropriate boundaries, set limits, and express negative emotions. In fact, one way to understand the assertiveness problem is as a technique for maintaining internal boundaries. Internal boundaries are the helpful guidelines we impose on ourselves to provide structure to our lives—for example, being in bed by 11:00 P.M. in order to get enough rest for the next day. Practice saying no to small things at first, like "I have to get off the phone now because it's getting late." Give yourself time to develop more sophisticated boundaries and assertiveness skills.

You may have already realized that a major trigger is activated when you feel compelled to say or do things that you aren't comfortable with, or when you have to act as though you feel something that you don't. You don't feel able or confident about how not to do what is being asked of you, so you do it, feel terrible, and then act out the resultant feelings. For example, your partner asks you to spend the weekend with his family, and you say yes even though you really need to stay home and rest after an exhausting two weeks of being overloaded. During the visit you complain and get into an argument with him over a bunch of little things. Developing and honing your ability to say no directly can put you back in control of yourself, eliminating the need to act out in these situations.

Replacing passive and aggressive communication with assertive communication requires a lifetime commitment. It's easy to revert to old patterns at times when you are under stress, such as when you're tired, hungry, afraid, angry, guilty, ashamed, or trying to do too much. Ask yourself what was going on that prevented you from being assertive. Remember that you have a right to make mistakes; learn from them rather than dwelling on them. Review your

DEVELOPING ASSERTIVENESS SKILLS

assertive rights. Explore your fears to make sure that they're realistic, and ask yourself whether it is worth it to you to be assertive in this situation. Focus on the constructive things you said or did, so that the next time that situation comes up you'll be more assertive. Ask yourself what assertiveness skills you could use the next time you're in that situation. Role-play communicating assertively in that situation in your mind or with a therapist or trusted friend. Include what you think your partner would say. Finally, when you anticipate a difficult situation, mentally role-play communicating assertively, including the other person's responses.

Chapter 5

Overcoming Your Anger

Anger can be an expensive luxury
Italian Proverb

What Is Anger?

The theories, research, and myths about anger are many and varied. Debate about the anger literature is not found in this book. Here you will find an approach to self-control of angry feelings for individuals seeking real relationships. Control of your anger feelings and hostility will help you be more connected to your partner and will probably improve your overall health.

The feeling of anger is a signal, a red flag telling us that you perceive something either not right or not fair. The angry feeling may mean that too much of your real self is being given up in the relationship, or that you perceive that your partner is taking advantage of you. Notice the word "perceive" here, which indicates that your perception and interpretation of an event or situation underlie the feelings of anger, not necessarily the real situation itself.

Sudden angry responses in relationships can be most helpfully understood as a defense against conscious or unconscious shame. Since for some partners the "spiraling down" feeling of shame is intolerable, anger and rage become responses that cover over the intolerable feelings. The angry partner is shouting a warning, "Don't get any closer to my pain! You are getting too close to my hidden sense of inadequacy, and I won't let anyone see that part of me. Stay away or I will attack." Partners are most apt to fly into an angry rage when surprised by a sudden attack on their identity. For example, you might offhandedly tell your partner that his clothes are too loud and nobody will want to talk to him at the dinner party you will both be attending. You may in fact be joking and not intending to hurt your partner. But he is hurt and responds angrily, "What do you mean, nobody will want to talk to me? People want to talk to me a whole lot more than they want to talk to you—at least I have some friends." Your partner feels intolerable shame and can only react to defend himself by cruelly attacking.

The first step in self-control and taking charge of ourselves and responsibility for our anger through understanding what happens when we feel angry. Let's take a closer look at anger as a process.

Angry Feelings as a Process

Angry feelings start with an experience of pain. The pain can be physical or emotional; it can be a stomachache or fatigue, feelings of rejection or loss. This pain causes a biological arousal, a strong desire for release. The emotional need deficits assessed in Chapter 1 can be used to predict potential pain experiences.

The second part in the progression of an angry feeling occurs when pain interacts with *beliefs*—assumptions about the cause of a painful experience. They are sometimes called *impulse beliefs* because they are quick, unquestioned, automatic. People tend to jump to impulsive conclusions about what hurts them. Sometimes the beliefs are accurate, like "Ow! I just got a paper cut." But in many cases the beliefs are incorrect, or at least exaggerated and distorted, like "She's doing that on purpose just to annoy me. It just goes to show how inconsiderate she is of my feelings." Such beliefs are considered shaming impulse beliefs for two reasons: they attempt to shame the other person or attribute blame, and they often arise out of unresolved feelings of shame within oneself. People with many distorted beliefs tend to become angry more easily than those with healthy, balanced belief systems.

Impulse beliefs of blame or condemnation toward your partner may be conscious (aware) or unconscious (unaware), and they function to ignite feelings of anger and discharge some of their arousal. Thus pain and arousal lead to blaming impulse beliefs, which lead to anger and more impulse beliefs and more anger in an escalating spiral. The beliefs and angry feelings can become a self-perpetuating loop. This self-perpetuating loop often keeps anger escalating for prolonged periods of time. It isn't possible to get angry without the presence of both painful arousal and impulse beliefs. Add into the mix a modern stressful lifestyle, and here lies an emotional explosion waiting to happen. In this chapter you will be given skills to control both stress and shaming impulse beliefs.

Angry Feelings Are Different from Aggressive Actions

Angry feelings are *emotions*. They occur when pain (feeling hurt), stress, or arousal combine with beliefs to create anger. Aggressive actions, by contrast, are *behaviors*. They are things you do, ways of interacting with your partner. Aggressive actions can be in the form of either physical or verbal assault. You can be angry without being aggressive and vice versa. Professional hit men are not necessarily angry when they pull the trigger; on the other hand, when you are angry, you can *choose not* to attack the person who is arousing your wrath.

Impulse Beliefs

Someone steps on your foot and you feel the pain. Your mind now interprets the event by retrieving a belief regarding the incident. What was the motive of the perpetrator? Is your belief that this was done on purpose to hurt you, or was it an innocent accident caused by the benign awkwardness of a time-pressured fellow commuter? Your belief will make the difference between intense hot anger and mild annoyance. Let's take a look at some common belief distortions that affect the impulse of angry feelings.

Basic Mistrust

Anger and hostility are often a result of basic mistrust of other people. The basic belief is that others in general, and your partner specifically, are selfish and/or mean. You may find yourself hypervigilant toward your partner's misbehavior. This belief will cause a great number of serious problems in your relationship.

Basic mistrust is detrimental to real relationships because you are forced into needing control. You need to control situations and your partner's behavior because you cannot trust that he or she will do the right thing.

If you have problems with basic mistrust, here are some sentences you can repeat to yourself that will help you overcome it. Repeating helpful reminders to yourself is called *self-talk*; this and anything else that helps you deal with a problem is called a *coping response*. As with all the coping responses in this book, you will need to repeat them quite a few times for them to sink in. You cannot undo a lifetime of basic mistrust or any other problem by just saying something once or twice. Be patient.

- Everyone makes the best possible choice given what he or she knows.

- Everyone uses the best problem-solving strategy available to him or her.
- I may not like it, but people are doing the best they can.
- No one is right or wrong. We just have different needs.
- I can relinquish control and let my partner take charge of some situations.

Shoulds

Anger is often the result of a judgment based on a set of rules about how people *should* and should not act. If you grew up a family with at least one parent who was quite critical, you have a good chance of having some belief distortions around shoulds. You have inevitably internalized the harsh critical aspect of your parents. The basic belief is that individuals who act according to the rules are right, and those who break the rules are wrong. Angry partners will think that the other knows and accepts their rules but deliberately chooses to violate them. The initial problem with shoulds, however, is that the other partner often disagrees with many of the rules.

Suppose Partner A is angry about shoulds. Her perception of the situation leaves her blameless and justified. Yet Partner B's rules consistently seem to offer protection from Partner B's viewpoint, so the partners feel that they are at an impasse. Another problem with shoulds is that Partner B *never* does what he should do from Partner A's viewpoint. He does only what is reinforcing and rewarding for him. In the end shoulds are one partner's values and needs imposed on the very different values and needs of the other.

Here are some coping responses to shoulds:

- What needs influence him or her to act this way?
- What problems, fears, or limits influence this behavior?
- What beliefs or values influence him/her to act this way?
- Forget the shoulds; they only get me upset.

- People do what *they* want to do or think they should do, not what *I* think they should do.

The Fantasy of Entitlement

The entitlement fantasy is based on a belief that when you want something badly enough, you ought to be given it. When a perceived need has great intensity, the demand that someone provide for it follows. The fantasy is that you are entitled to things in life, and when you don't get them, your partner is depriving you. There is confusion between wish and requirement. It seems for entitled partners that their wishing for something means it is unacceptable for their partner to say no.

Entitlement is destructive to real relationships. It requires that your wish come first and that your partner must submit. Sometimes one partner expects that the other partner give up his or her real self. Entitled partners may be gratified for a while but this usually will not last.

Here are some statements for entitled partners:

1. I am free to wish for things, but you are free to say no.
2. My wish doesn't require you to meet it.
3. I have my needs and you have your needs.
4. I have my limits and you have your limits.
5. If I wish for something, it's ultimately my responsibility to get it, not yours.

The Fantasy of Unconditional Correctness

The fantasy of unconditional correctness resides in the belief that there is an absolute model of correct human behavior. It is believed that human beings ought to know and follow this model. Applied to relationships, partners who hold this fantasy keep an emotional scorecard logging strikes for and against each partner. Unfortunately no two partners agree on what correctness is. Correctness becomes a totally subjective concept, depending completely on what each partner expects, needs, or wishes for from the other. Since the model of correctness is ultimately a result of each partner's respective beliefs and emotional need deficits, each partner can call literally anything correct or incorrect. Telling a partner he or she is incorrect will add fuel to the conflict.

Partners who have the fantasy of unconditional correctness can use the following statements:

1. We each have different needs, and they are equally important.
2. Each need is valid, and we can compromise and negotiate.
3. We each have different experiences and backgrounds.

Exaggeration Words

The use of exaggeration words like "horrifying," "disaster," "awful," "appalling," or "horrendous" have a negative effect in resolving conflict. A partner may overstate situations by using words such as "always," "all," "every," "never." For example, "She never cleans up after herself." "He's horrendous with everybody." "She is never helpful." These exaggerations increase the sense of negativity and anxiety within the listener. Exaggeration of the situation also increases a sense of victimization. "You're bad and I'm an innocent victim."

Partners who use exaggeration words can remember these statements:

1. Forget "always" or "never."
2. Forget exaggerations.
3. The facts, just the facts.
4. Be accurate.

Shaming Statements

Shaming statements are general negative judgments and character attacks. Categorizing your partner as ridiculous, bad, stupid, selfish, or lazy are ways to say that he or she is unacceptable or inadequate. Shaming statements can escalate your anger by categorizing your partner as worthless or incompetent, not deserving of respect. The whole person is rejected rather than a disapproved-of behavior. One character trait of your partner becomes who he or she is. Placing your partner into a category undeserving of respect allows you to feel angry more easily.

A partner who uses shaming statements can recall these phrases:

1. Nobody is all bad. My partner is doing the best he or she can at the moment.
2. Forget character attacks.
3. Focus on the present problem behavior.

Dealing with Anger: Coping Works Better Than Shaming

All painful and hurtful situations offer a choice. You can choose to shame your partner for the event, or you can use cognitive skills and/or relaxation techniques to reduce your angry feelings and talk about your needs in a nonshaming fashion. If you tell your partner that she is lazy for not doing her chores, it may really feel good for a minute to get it off your chest. But the situation will likely escalate from there. You both may end up raising voices, and the relationship may spiral downward. Skill practice will allow you to make another choice. You can decide to use some relaxation techniques to lower your stress level, to alter some of your impulse beliefs, and/or talk to your partner in a nonshaming way about the problem. For example, even if you feel angry inside, you deliberately take a few minutes to relax first and then say calmly, "I'd really like to see the house look neater than this before Don and Judy come over tonight. If I vacuum the carpets, could you clean up the kitchen sometime before five o'clock?" This approach is almost guaranteed to get a better result than flying into a rage and shouting, "You lazy slob! This house always looks like a dump! Why can't you get your act together? I bet if I smash this vase you won't even clean it up."

Venting Is Not Ultimately Effective

Our culture typically encourages people to get in touch with their anger and to "get it out." The belief that venting anger is helpful is a piece of the truth. Venting anger may help a person initially feel better. However, I've had many people report to me that there is a loss of self-esteem as well. Venting anger provides some initial gratification, but this may soon be followed by the realization of loss of control and a sense of inadequacy. Research shows that venting can even make you angrier at times, because you replay all the dastardly things that your partner may have "done to you." It concentrates your beliefs about your partner's wrongs and your sense of having been victimized. Venting can actually serve to prolong anger and may also make it easier to get angry again in the future because you have solidified your beliefs.

Calm Yourself with Muscle Relaxation

Learning to relax in provocative situations can calm you down sufficiently so that you can more clearly think of ways to handle the conflict.
1. Make a fist with each hand and squeeze tight. Really concentrate on the feeling of tension in your fists and forearms. Hold for several seconds. Now relax. Feel the difference in your muscles. Notice a heaviness, warmth,

tingling, or whatever relaxation feels like for you. Now raise your arms and tighten them, flexing your biceps. Hold the tension for seven seconds, and then let your arms fall limp by your sides. Once again notice feelings of relaxation, warmth, or heaviness spreading through your arms as you let them drop. Really notice the contrast between tension and relaxation in your arms.
2. Now turn your attention to your upper face. Frown, squint your eyes shut as hard as you can, and hold for seven seconds. Relax, and notice what it feels like to let go of tension in your upper face. Now tighten your jaw (not so hard that you'll crack a tooth) and push your tongue up against the roof of your mouth. Hold it for seven seconds. And relax. Notice what it feels like for your jaw to let go and be really loose. Now tense your neck muscles by shrugging your shoulders upward as far as you can (but don't try to pull your neck in like a turkey.) Wait a moment and relax. Let the relaxation move from your shoulders and neck up to your jaw and all the way to your forehead.
3. Now move your awareness to your chest and back. Take a deep breath and hold it. Tense your chest, shoulders, and upper back muscles, making your entire upper torso rigid. Take another deep breath. After seven seconds, let out the breath with a long, loud sigh, and let your torso go limp. Really melt down into the chair and focus on the difference between the tense and the relaxed states.
4. Now move your attention downward—into your stomach, lower back, and pelvic regions. Tighten your stomach, lower back, and buttocks slowly. After seven seconds, relax and melt again into the chair. Notice feelings of warmth or heaviness spreading throughout your abdomen.
5. Now work on your legs. With your toes pointed straight out, like a ballerina, tense your thighs, your calves, and your feet. Hold this for seven seconds, then let your legs

totally relax. Feel the heaviness and warmth flood into your legs as they go limp. Now tense your legs again, this time, pulling your toes up toward your head. Hold for seven seconds and let the relaxation spread like a wave throughout your entire body, into your abdomen and your chest, into your arms, your neck, your face and forehead, until you feel totally relaxed. Take another deep breath.

Calm Yourself with Visualization

You will now identify a special relaxation image. Picture yourself in a calm, peaceful place. Make sure that all your major senses are involved. You should be able to see the shapes and colors, hear the sounds, feel the temperature and textures of the special place. If there are smells and tastes, include these also. Work carefully on constructing the image, developing as much detail as possible. Make sure that the image is capable of eliciting the emotion of contentment, safety, and calmness.

1. Think about a place where you've felt especially safe, relaxed, or content. It could be the beach, mountains, meadows, your childhood bedroom, or a remembered moment of deep relaxation and peace. It can be a real place, or you could just make one up. Close your eyes and try to see the shapes and colors of your place. Hear the sounds of your place; hear birds, waves, or babbling water. Feel the temperature of your place—is it cool or warm? Feel the textures of whatever you touch in your special place.
2. Make sure that everything in your special place makes you feel relaxed and safe. Change anything that doesn't feel right. If you want to add some trees, put them in. If you want the sound of a waterfall, add it. If you want to be alone, take the people out of your scene. If you want your dog, put him in.

3. Now use your special place visualization quickly, almost like a reflex, when things get stressful. Go ahead and visualize your special place. Construct the scene as quickly as you can; really get into it until you feel the peacefulness, the safety, the relaxation. [Pause one minute.] Now get ready to leave the scene. Open your eyes and look around. Notice the environment. [Pause.] Now close your eyes again and return to your special place. See it, hear it, feel it, let it surround you and touch each of your senses. [Pause.] Now come back to the room and take a quick look at the environment again. [Pause.] One last time go back to the special place. Get there as quickly as you can, let it bathe your senses, see its shapes and colors, hear the sounds, feel it in your skin. [Pause.] Now come back to the room. You can go to your special place anytime you need to relax, to get out of a situation that provokes or disturbs you.

Self-Talk Phrases for Angry Moments

It can be helpful to maintaining self-control by repeating the following phrases:

- *Everyone makes the best possible choice given what he or she knows right now.*
- *Everyone uses the best problem-solving strategy available to him or her right now.*
- *I may not like it, but the other person is doing the best he or she can.*
- *No one is right or wrong. We just have different needs.*
- *I can stay calm and relaxed.*
- *Take a deep breath and relax.*
- *I'm not going to let him or her get to me.*
- *Just as long as I stay calm, I'm in control.*
- *I can't change him or her with anger; I'll just upset myself.*

- *Getting upset and angry won't help, although it might feel good for the short term.*
- *I can find a way to say what I want to without anger.*
- *Forget the shoulds; they just get me upset.*
- *People do what they want to do, not what I think they should do.*
- *I can say no, and so can my partner.*
- *I'm allowed to have needs, and so is my partner.*
- *Each partner's need is legitimate—we can negotiate*
- *My desire doesn't obligate my partner to fulfill it. Our needs are equally important.*
- *People change only when it is reinforced and encouraged, and they are capable of changing.*
- *People change only when they want to.*
- *I'm not helpless. I can take care of myself in this situation.*
- *Don't second-guess the motives of others.*
- *Assume nothing—or else check out every assumption.*
- *No more "always" or "never."*
- *No more "all or nothing."*
- *No more shaming.*
- *Accuracy, not exaggeration.*
- *No mean labels.*
- *No sarcasm, no attacks.*
- *No matter what is said, I know I'm a good person.*

Healthy Separateness

Partners can find that their dependency on each other is out of balance and the cause of much conflict. Taking charge of yourself is a primary principle in real relationships. When you are angry with your partner for not doing a task around the house or elsewhere, simply do it yourself. You obviously feel stronger about the task, and it makes sense to take responsibility for your own needs. Yvonne, after months of reminders and several heated discussions, was angry with Keith because he would not take care of the broken garage door opener. She finally realized that she cared more about the problem than he did and could call the door-opener company herself and get it repaired. Taking charge of yourself includes determining whose need it really is and realizing that it is often healthier to do it yourself.

It is not reasonable to expect one person to fulfill all of your needs. Your partner has different needs, wants, and interests. Letting go of the expectation that your partner must meet certain needs will help create a more balanced relationship. To expect him or her to do something because it is your priority is to remain in a "no difference" fantasy. Within appropriate reason, you can go elsewhere to meet your needs. You take charge of yourself as you find sources of nurture and support rather than rely completely on your partner.

If you consistently are urged by your partner to do things you know you don't want to do, it is important to say no sometimes. If you don't say no, you may end up being resentful and acting it out. Limit setting is an important aspect of taking charge of yourself and your needs. Asking directly for what you want is a significant way to take charge of yourself. Assertively negotiating for your needs without anger or blame is helpful especially when you have experienced resentment for having given your partner more than you get. (See Chapter 9 on basic conflict resolution skills.)

Expressing Limits: Saying No

Many angry partners find it difficult to express limits and say no. They may have a tendency to agree readily to the other partner's expressed needs or requests and later feel resentful. Once they realize that they have overcommitted to meeting the other partner's needs, they become angry. They now condemn the other partner's needs rather than their own difficulty in saying no. Getting in touch with the fact that you have limits and cannot do everything without later feeling taken advantage of and resentful is a necessary aspect of taking responsibility for your anger. For more discussion on saying no, see Chapter 4.

You have already seen that a major anger trigger is activated when you feel compelled to say or do things that you aren't comfortable, or when you have to act as though you feel something that you don't. You don't feel able or confident about how not to do what is being asked of you, so you do it, feel terrible, and then act out of anger. Developing and refining your ability to say no directly can put you back in control of yourself, eliminating the need to act out in these situations.

You may feel that "what's done is done". Often you *can* go back and "fix" a situation by expressing your feelings to the person who was initially involved in the interaction. No one expects that you'll always express yourself perfectly the first time. Most people are willing to hear you out, even if it's about something that happened quite awhile ago. You can achieve two benefits from doing this. First, you might very well resolve a conflict with someone and feel better about him or her and yourself. Second, by practicing going back and resolving old grievances, you will gradually develop the ability to confront issues as they happen.

Setbacks

The reduction of feelings of anger is not the hallmark of a successful or complete recovery. As you mature emotionally, you develop healthier coping mechanisms that take the place of the anger problem. Remember when your anger control problem relapses, you will have broken through a wall of your own creation that was protecting you.

The protective wall is now not nearly as strong as it

was before you crashed through it because you are now involved in the old impulse beliefs and behavior. It is important to go over exactly what happened and how the old impulse beliefs came to the forefront. A working through of excessive shame is not done overnight. Be aware of the fact that you are susceptible to further slips. You will need to make an extra effort to review this chapter.

1. Contact people you trust and let them know about your slip. Your honesty with them will help you be honest with yourself and promote your healing.
2. Reestablish a relaxation and anxiety-reduction program.
3. Begin by repeating appropriate self-talk phrases.
4. Identify any significant belief distortions that trigger the anger and develop appropriate responses.
5. Consider doing more significant work with a competent psychotherapist or psychoanalyst experienced in the area of anger and shame.

Chapter 6

Overcoming Your Partner's Anger

"Come, come, you wasp; i' faith, you are too angry."
—Petruchio to Kate, *Taming of the Shrew*

Most partners who are habitually angry cannot effectively communicate what is going on for them internally. They do not possess the skills to sufficiently articulate their thoughts or feelings in conflict situations. They don't know the skills of setting limits, basic conflict resolution, or support cooperation. Shaming messages are the usual response to psychological threat and lack of personal coping skills.

Shaming messages are painful, especially from someone with whom you are emotionally connected. Unfortunately these messages can rekindle old early experiences of being shamed by family or childhood peers. When your partner is angry and responds through attacks or criticisms, you can feel justified in responding with your own anger. However, this will just escalate the situation.

How to Handle Several Types of Angry, Shaming Behavior

The bad news is that angry partners can send shaming messages to you in a number of ways. The good news is that there are specific strategies you can use to handle each situation and help your partner resolve conflict more constructively. Let's take a look at some ways your partner may send shaming messages to you and how to deal with it.

Depriving You of an Emotional Need

Your partner's message is designed to deprive you of a nurturing emotional need. The intentional taking away of something you need is used to control the situation but carries with it the extreme cost of your resentment and mistrust. For example, your partner says, "I'm too tired to go out to dinner tonight at the neighbors' house" following your reluctance to "spend the money right now" during a discussion of his desire to purchase a $40,000 sport utility vehicle. Interpretation: You say no to the SUV, so I will deprive you of going out to dinner together.

It is likely that you are dealing a partner who possesses narcissistic personality qualities. There are two theories from which the narcissistic character type is derived: (1) from early deprivation, (2) from having been doted on in early life. It is likely that both theories are correct, as the early life may have yielded the experience of both grandiosity and worthlessness.

The Story of Narcissus

The ancient Greeks tell us that Narcissus was a handsome young man. Dozens of maidens and nymphs loved him, but he was uninterested in any of them. Instead, as a punishment for all the hearts he had broken, an angry goddess made him fall in love with the reflection of his own image in a pool, and he remained transfixed and immobile there until some magical transformation wrought by the gods changed him into a lovely, fragrant white flower that will always bloom as winter gives way to spring. If we assume that Narcissus' fate was a bad outcome, we are led to conclude that his fault lay in having fallen in love with the image of himself, sacrificing his ties to the world in favor of the relief from emotional pain offered by loving the one lover who never leaves...himself.

People with the narcissistic character type seek to preserve an original blissful state by viewing themselves as special. This personality type has a strong need for positive mirroring in order to maintain the self-idealization. It is helpful to remember that this way of being in the world is a defense for woundedness.

The risk in dealing with narcissistic people is that they will easily split. Your partner can appear to idealize you initially, but watch out when you express the need for a limit and thus no longer offer enough positive mirroring. As idealized as you may have been, you will now be deprecated as the narcissist becomes enraged or withdraws completely. Nor will the withdrawal be the end; a narcissistic partner will likely retaliate in some hurtful way.

Dealing with your partner requires strategies for working around the splitting. Avoid going head to head. You may simply have to wait it out until the rage subsides and your partner realizes (in the earlier example about the SUV) that he or she to wants to go out for dinner. Allow someone who is idealized by your partner to help you by suggesting the benefits of your point of view to your partner. When your partner's rage has subsided, you can ask your partner what he or she thinks the two of you should do for dinner that night. Deep down inside, your partner may very well want to go out for dinner after all. Alternatively, you may want to point out how your partner will look better if he or she shows up for dinner.

Applying Guilt

Your partner's messages are intended to suggest that you are morally inadequate for not providing his or her needs. You may feel as if you are wrong, being mean, or without normal human consideration for having a different need. For example, "I've spent the whole week at work trying provide for the family, and you can't even put away my clean clothes in the drawer for me? You are the most inconsiderate person I've ever met." Interpretation: You are selfish because you don't take care of my needs.

Your partner may have aggressive character qualities. He or she has a strong sense of how others ought to think and act. There are lots of oughts and shoulds. When these expectations are not met, direct or indirect cutting attacks toward you become his or her mode of operation.

The primary strategy for dealing with your partner is to refuse to fulfill his or her expectation that, through either fear or rage, you will be put out of commission. Your partner will continue the same behavior only if it still works. You must initially, however, avoid an open confrontation over who is right or who will be the winner. Therefore you need to give your partner time to run down but also stand your ground. Get your partner's attention by standing or calling him or her by name. Don't worry about being polite, get in however you can. If possible, get your partner to sit down. Maintain eye contact. State your own opinions and perceptions forcefully, but don't argue with your partner's opinions or put them down. Be ready to be friendly.

Invalidating Your Needs

Your partner's message is that your needs are inappropriate or without merit. Your needs are deemed as illegitimate or less important than his or hers. For example, "When we visit your mother in Florida, all we ever do are projects or tasks around the house. We never even take time out to relax. At least with my family, we discuss different things and relate. It's a real family, not just work." Interpretation: Your need for your mother is not as valid as my need for my family.

Your partner could have some features of a complaining character. He or she may demonstrate a sometimes whining quality that self-righteously blames and accuses. You may find yourself automatically placating or becoming defensive with your partner, even if you have not done anything wrong. Complaining partners are not just confronting legitimate problems with the complaining; while there may be a kernel of truth to the problem raised, the fact that they blame outside of themselves is a telltale sign. There is little responsibility taken for their own part in difficulties.

Complaining partners do not experience themselves as whining. They are focused on something gone wrong that someone else must fix. They see themselves as powerless. They may feel powerless in the management of their own lives, as if the cause of all that happens to them lies outside their grasp. This passive view may attribute all that goes well to good fortune or favors received from others. Your partner has a sense of how things should be and a strong sense of injustice and that they are not that way. Your partner probably sees himself or herself as rather perfect, at least most of the time. Complaining keeps your partner blameless, innocent, and morally superior. This way of being in a relationship does not really work well, however, because while complaining gets attention, it rarely gets the behavior response they seek.

Deal with your partner by listening attentively to his or her complaints, as difficult as this may be. Acknowledge what your partner is saying by reflecting it back to him or her. Don't agree with or apologize for the complaints even if, at the moment, you believe them to be true. Dodge the accusation by avoiding defensiveness and escalating the conflict. Tell the facts as you see them without additional comment. Use a problem-solving approach by asking specific informational questions and brainstorming options. If all else fails ask your partner, "How do you want this discussion to end?"

Threatening to Leave

Some partners convey the message that if you don't submit to their demands, they will either emotionally withdraw or in some way abandon you. This threat may be so intolerable to you that you comply. A pattern can develop that is very unhealthy to the relationship. For example, following your statement that you have had a particularly tiring day and would like to go to sleep early, your partner replies, "This relationship is not working. If you are not even willing to have sex with me, I don't know why we are even together. I'm out of here." Interpretation: If you don't give up your need for rest, I'm going to abandon you.

Your partner may have qualities of a tantrum-type aggressive character. This is a difficult personality to deal with because the threat to leave throws you off balance and often forces you to give your partner what he or she wants. The style is to explode periodically through tantrums. If you have sensitivity to abandonment issues, this form of manipulation creates in you a "do anything to appease" response. However, the resentment that builds up becomes a major problem.

When you express your limits, consciously or unconsciously, your partner sometimes responds by throwing a tantrum because he or she cannot tolerate the psychological threat of being told no. You may be totally unaware of having said anything wrong, so it takes you by surprise, further throwing you off balance.

Deal with your partner's tantrum by remembering that he or she will need extra time to cool down and regain self-control. You can excuse yourself or disappear for awhile by going and doing something you find relaxing and helpful in managing your anxiety about the threatened separation. Offer to return later to talk about the issue. Or you may need to shout, "Stop!" to break the tantrum if it becomes a tirade. When your partner has regained some control, attempt to show that you take your partner seriously. Try to discuss the difference of needs in a calm way.

Threatening Harmful Consequences

Some partners make it clear that if you do not comply with their demands, they will act out something hurtful to you. This is an extreme and costly control technique that results in resentment and destruction of the relationship. For example, "Well, if you aren't interested in helping me out with this, maybe I'll ask Kathy (former lover) if she would help me out." Interpretation: Give me what I want or I will flirt with the rekindling of a former romance.

Your partner is aggressively using the emotional ammunition of jealousy in order to manipulate you to give something beyond your limit. Your partner may have an aggressive character structure, which features a strong need to prove that his or her view of the world is the correct one. This type of personality comes out charging like a bull. Such people may be emotionally abusive, physically abrupt, or simply intimidating and overwhelming. When you resist your partner's plans, the response is irritation or outright rage. Your partner takes his or her needs very seriously.

Again, the basic strategy for dealing with your partner's aggressive qualities is to not fulfill his or her expectations. Your partner will continue to behave in a bullying manner only if it works. You must, however, avoid an open confrontation over who is right or who is to be the winner. Give your partner time to cool off, but stand your ground. State your position, do not comment on your partner's position, and be ready to find a solution.

Calling You Names or Putting You Down

Your partner's put-down messages or name calling are degrading to your character and may be intended to make you feel foolish or inappropriate for having a difference in needs from him or her. For example, "Your stupid family doesn't have a whole brain between them. Why do we have to visit them on the holidays this year? It just won't work!" Interpretation: Your family is worthless, so don't have any needs to connect with them.

Your partner uses negativity as a tool for control. This is a very primitive response void of empathy and reasonableness. People with negative character qualities often use pessimistic statements like, "It just won't work" or "It's no use trying because we already tried that last year." When in this state of mind, your partner believes that there is no way of fixing problems, there can be no resolution. Your partner may have a profound impact on your state of mind, because you can feel helpless in the midst of his or her negativity.

Your partner gains power over you by tapping into your potential for despair. Such partners believe at times that forces in the world are absolute, not just issues to be worked through. They may be convinced that they have little power over their own lives. They may be subject to "all or nothing" thinking and fail to realize that although they don't have full power to shape their destiny, they do have some power to influence their lives. Your partner may also see authority figures as demons or gods, rather than ordinary fallible persons.

The most important first step in dealing with this type of partner is to be alert to your own potential for being drawn into despair. Once you have dealt with yourself, do not try to argue your partner out of his or her pessimism. That will just strengthen your partner's resolve. Let the problem be fully discussed, let your partner get all the negativity out before offering solutions or alternatives. Anticipate the negative possibilities and preempt them as potential problems to overcome. Beware of creating negativism with highly analytical negative partners by eliciting responses to act before they are ready. Be prepared to go at it alone in a situation if necessary.

Saying Yes but Meaning No

Your partner's message is agreeable but confuses the focus from your need to some other "more significant" subject. This is something like invalidating your needs but with a spin, discussed in Chapter 4. Here is an example: "OK, OK, you want me to help out more with the child care. I'll take care of it. I've got a total meltdown at the office with this new senior vice president coming in and telling everybody to rewrite their job descriptions. My mother called earlier and wants us to come over for dinner Sunday. Did you bring in the mail?" Interpretation: I'm very agreeable to helping you with your needs. I really don't want to discuss it. Unfortunately, nothing happens and there is no physical response.

Such partners are agreeable and friendly, which may be their primary goal in life. They are quite likable and seem very responsive. What you want, you get—until you need some action or an honest, tough-minded discussion of a problem. They leave you believing they are in agreement with your plan, only to let you down when some action by them is required. The shaming message here is subtle: you are worth agreeing with, but your ideas are not worth following through with action. Your partner will often use humor as a way to ease tension. It is usually intended as an expression of intimacy, but it can also be a way of sending a shaming message.

This type of partner may have the ultra-agreeable character quality of a strong need to be liked and accepted. Such partners may be very proficient in making you feel liked and acceptable much of the time. They give to others what they need. There is another side, however, because all conflict is quite uncomfortable for them, and conflict inevitably occurs when their need for approval collides with negative aspects of reality. Rather than directly face the risk of losing your approval, your partner will commit himself or herself to your plan or needs without being able or willing to follow through.

The most important task in dealing with this kind of partner is to surface the underlying facts and issues that prevent your partner from taking action. Let your partner know that you value him or her as a person by saying so directly. Next, ask your partner to tell you about those things that might interfere with your real relationship. Ask your partner to talk about any aspect of the plan or action to be taken that could possibly be a problem. Be ready to compromise and negotiate if open conflict is in the wind. Listen to your partner's humor. There may be significant messages in those teasing remarks.

Ask for a Healthy Time-Out

Calling for a healthy time-out before anger escalates into the destructive zone is an effective skill for dealing with an angry partner. Anger levels within the reasonable zone will allow for expression of thoughts and feelings necessary for conflict resolution. When the level gets too high, anxiety will also rise, and you and your partner can quickly become unreasonable in discussing issues. Tempers will flare, and destructive shaming ensues.

Initiating a healthy time-out requires monitoring both your and your partner's anger levels. Awareness of the signs of escalating anger can be determined and used to signal the initiation of a helpful break in the action. Signs may include shouting, excessive cursing and name calling, and physical or emotional threats, as well as obvious shaming and blaming statements. If either of your anger levels approaches the destructive zone, it is appropriate to call for a halt in the discussion. The time-out will allow for the level of anger to decrease and reasonableness to return.

You and your partner should discuss and agree on the use of healthy time-outs. It is vital to agree that if only one of you wants a healthy time-out, that is sufficient to require it. It is also important to agree on the warning signs of potentially destructive anger levels. A "healthy time-out signal," like the "T" used by basketball or football players in order to stop the clock, is also helpful.

The purpose of the healthy time-out is to protect the relationship from becoming destructive and shaming. It is not appropriate to call a time-out because you want to punish your partner by withholding communication or resolution. For the sake of the relationship, you will postpone the discussion to a time when you are both calmer and more reasonable. It is appropriate to call for a healthy time-out following your partner's statement rather than your own. Tell your partner, "I need a healthy time-out right now, and we can continue this when I get back from going out for a breather." You have directly stated your need and your intention to return to the discussion when the two of you are calmer. If your partner does not agree quickly, repeat the words, "healthy time-out" and leave the room or area. You are taking personal responsibility for your anger and the overall health of the relationship.

Chapter 7

Overcoming Your Anxiety

How much has cost us the evils that never happened!
Thomas Jefferson

Anxiety Threatens Real Relationships

As with anger, the research and theories about anxiety are vast and diverse. Discussion about the anxiety literature is not found in this book. Here you will find an approach to anxiety management for individuals seeking real relationships. Coping with your feelings of anxiety will help you to relate to your partner in a healthier way.

Feelings of anxiety in relationships may manifest in unnecessary conflict and miscommunication. Anxiety is the feeling of being overwhelmed, enfeebled, or fragmented. It is consciously experienced as fear, worry, or nervousness. Anxiety arises when either partner experiences doubt regarding his or her ability to handle an event or situation. A partner's knowledge of the anxiety experience may be conscious or unconscious. How partners individually react to the feeling of anxiety can result in conflict for the couple. For example, Partner A is going on a business trip the next morning and comes home from a hard day of work to spend some relaxing time with Partner B. Both partners have childhood issues with separation, and they experience anxiety around the business trip. Partner A tends to react to anxiety by having a few drinks before and during dinner.

Partner B reacts by complaining about unfinished tasks around the house. A nasty argument ensues. The partners in this example were not very aware of feeling anxiety regarding the business trip. Not until several months later, after the situation repeated itself several times, did they realize that the separation was triggering the nasty arguments.

It is helpful to recognize that anxiety at one level is simply the result of the renowned fight-or-flight response. This is a natural bodily response that enables human beings to be alerted to and quickly flee a truly dangerous situation. What makes anxiety difficult to cope with is that the intense reaction often occurs in the absence of any immediate or apparent danger. When there is no apparent, external danger in anxiety, it often remains unconscious. Your mind can very quickly go through the process: "If I feel this bad, it must be my partner's fault."

You may have a belief that heart palpitations will lead to a heart attack, that your constricted breathing will lead to suffocation, or that you will lose control and "go crazy." The truth is that none of these ever occurs. It is not possible to have a heart attack as a result of anxiety. The human heart is made of very strong and dense muscle fibers. A healthy heart can beat over 200 beats per minute for days—even weeks—without sustaining any damage. Electrocardiogram tracings of high levels of anxiety have shown rapid heartbeat without any of the types of abnormalities associated with individuals who have heart conditions. Nor can you suffocate from anxiety. Your brain has an automatic reflex mechanism that will force you to breathe if you're not getting enough oxygen. Dizziness may manifest because of reduced circulation to the brain during high levels of anxiety, but you will not faint. Depth breathing can relieve the sensations precipitating these symptoms. Anxiety has never caused anyone lose control or to "go crazy." Although anxiety is uncomfortable for a time, it is not dangerous.

Early Signs of Anxiety

You can learn to recognize early signs of anxiety. You may be signaled by awareness of an increase in heartbeat. Or you might become conscious of a tightening in the chest, sweaty skin, or butterflies in your gut. Many people experience some type of preliminary signs before higher levels of anxiety become evident. It's possible to recognize different levels of anxiety by using the Anxiety Table.

Table 2: *Anxiety Table*

7-10 Major Anxiety	The same symptoms in 'Marked Anxiety' magnified; fear of going crazy or dying; terror, obsession with escape.
6 Marked Anxiety	Quite difficult to breathe; palpitations; disorientation or dissociation (unreality as mind goes someplace else); compounding fear arises in response to perceived loss of control.
5 Moderate Anxiety	Heart pounding quite rapidly or beating irregularly/abruptly; constricted breathing; "zoned out" or dizziness; real fear of losing control; compelled to escape.
4 Low Anxiety	Feeling uncomfortable or beginning to "zone out," heart beating rapidly; muscles tightening; worry about maintaining control.
3 Slight Anxiety	Feeling awkward but still in control; heart starting to beat more rapidly; slightly sweaty skin.
2 Early Anxiety	Butterflies in gut; muscle tension, moderately nervous.
1 Very Early Anxiety	Passing 'glimmer' of anxiety; feeling slightly nervous.
0 No Anxiety	Feeling of well being and at peace.

The symptoms described in the Anxiety Table may be varied. Each individual has his or her own unique set of signs and symptoms that will manifest prior to the point where a sense of control seems lost.

External Causes of Anxiety

Some factors that contribute to anxiety originate from outside a person and create a sense of internal chaos.

Parents Who Were Overly Critical and/or Had Excessively High Standards

Children who experience critical and/or perfectionistic parents are never quite sure of their acceptability. As adults they may be overly eager to please, look good, and be nice at the expense of their owjn needs and feelings. Early experiences of insecurity lead to dependency or restriction from some activities or social situations where there is a possibility of losing face or appearing unacceptable. (See Chapter 3 on overcoming the power of shame.)

Families with Emotional Insecurity and Dependency

Several kinds of diffiucult family situations can lead to deep-seated insecurity. The loss of a parent through death or divorce can cause strong fears of abandonment in a child. Rejection, physical or sexual abuse, neglect, or family alcoholism can also generate insecurity. A child's response to his or her insecurity will commonly result in unhealthy dependency with associated anxiety features.

Cumulative Stress

Stress can accumulate over time as a result of long-standing family or interpersonal problems. It can accumulate as the result of many major life transitions within a short period of time, such as marriage or divorce, change of job or geographic relocation, health issues, or financial changes. If stress isn't managed well, it will accumulate. The long-term effects of stress can be diverse. Chronic headaches, ulcers, high blood pressure, and depression are all manifestations of cumulative stress on the body.

Internal Causes of Anxiety

Some causes of anxiety originate inside a person. Internal dynamics contribute to an increased sense of chaos and increase anxiety.

Anxious Distorted-Belief Phrases

Belief phrases are what you say to yourself in your own mind. Most people engage in an internal monologue much of the time. However, it may be so automatic and subtle that you are unaware (unconscious) of it—and of how distorted some of your automatic belief phrases may be—until a qualified psychotherapist helps you explore them. Remarks you make to yourself starting with the words "What if," for example, "What if I can't handle this?" generate much of your anxiety. "What if I lose control of my emotions when I talk to my partner about this?" "What if my partner rejects me if I reveal this about myself?" Anxious distorted-belief phrases expect inadequacy in advance. It is an issue of mistrust of yourself or your partner. This type of thinking is usually called worry. The good news is that you can learn to recognize anxious distorted-belief phrases, stop them, and replace them with more helpful and soothing affirmations. There is a list of sample affirmations later in this chapter, and you may think of others that are especially helpful to you.

Pushing Down Feelings

Pushing down feelings of anger, sadness, frustration, excitement, or joy may generate what is known as free-floating anxiety. Free-floating anxiety is experienced as you feel vaguely anxious without having any clues to where it comes from. When you let out your angry feelings in a non-shaming manner, such as, "I feel angry when you don't take out the garbage at night because I end up having to do it in the morning," rather than, "You never do anything around here, you lazy slob," you will feel more at peace and less bottled up with negative emotion. Expression of feelings can have a positive effect on reducing general levels of anxiety.

Inadequate Assertive Communication Skills

Verbally expressing feelings to your partner requires the development of assertive communication skills. Assertive communication is the direct expression of thoughts and feelings in a forthright manner. It involves a healthy middle ground between submissiveness and aggressiveness. Partners who have tendencies toward anxiety often act submissively. They tend to avoid asking directly for their needs and are uncomfortable with the expression of strong feelings, especially anger. Frequently these partners are skittish about imposing on others or not being a "nice person." They fear that assertive communication will alienate their partner, whom they may depend on for their sense of cohesiveness and security. Development of assertive communication skills is essential to healthy management of anxiety.

Inadequate Self-Care Skills

A pervasive sense of insecurity is common to the psyche of many people with anxiety issues. Insecurity can arise from a variety of childhood experiences, such as parental neglect, abandonment, abuse, overprotection, and perfectionism, as well as from patterns of alcoholism or chemical dependency in the family. As a result of not having received consistent or reliable emotional support as children, as adults such people often lack the skills to adequately take care of their own needs. Without skills to love and nurture themselves, they suffer from low self-esteem and may feel anxious or overwhelmed in the face of adult demands and responsibilities. This lack of self-care skills increases and maintains their feelings of anxiety. The real solution for those who experienced inadequate parenting skills as a child is to be diligent toward parenting themselves as adults. For example, if you did not receive adequate physical nurture as a child, you can provide special self-care by taking extra time bathing and nurturing your own body. Or if you did not receive enough emotional support as child, you can spend time meditating or giving yourself affirmations.

Driven Lifestyle

Slowing down and not having to always be doing something will help reduce your susceptibility to anxiety. Practicing the skills for relaxation, exercise, altering distorted-belief phrases and mistaken beliefs, appropriate expression of feelings, assertive communication, and self-care will all contribute to helping you reduce the sources of anxiety in your life.

Inadequate Life Purpose

Partners who are aware of their life as having meaning, purpose, and a sense of direction tend to have lower levels of anxiety. Feelings of boredom or a sense of unfulfilled apathy are frequently prevalent when a partner has not discovered an enlivening reason for being. A sense of apathy can be a potent breeding ground for anxiety. An inadequate life purpose can be the basis for a cycle of depression and anger as well.

Poor Nutrition and Smoking

You undoubtedly know that good nutrition contributes to good health, but you may not realize that your eating and drinking habits have a profound influence on your overall level of anxiety. Excess caffeine, for example, can lead to increased levels of anxiety. And during anxious times, your body may need higher levels of vitamin C, the B vitamins, and other essentials to maintain your tolerance of anxiety and your ability to cope. Low levels of nutrients have also been linked to anxiety-related symptoms such as insomnia, irritability, depression, and fatigue. Poor nutrition may well be one of the most neglected determinants of disabling anxiety. Minimizing the use of stimulants, sugar, alcohol, and processed foods will contribute to improved anxiety management.

Many people who smoke cigarettes report that smoking helps them relax and alleviates their feelings of anxiety and stress. However, Andrew Parrott, a psychologist at the University of East London, has recently argued that although smokers probably do not realize it, cigarette smoking actually *causes* stress. A review of the research on cigarette smoking and stress is consistent with this assertion. Smokers on average have higher levels of stress than do nonsmokers. When people quit smoking, they experience reduced levels of anxiety.

Skills for Overcoming Your Anxiety

Many people experience anxiety originating from one more of the external or internal sources listed above. Stress management through relaxation, exercise, good nutrition, time management and organization, social support, withdrawal from high-anxiety situations, redirecting attention, and adopting low-stress beliefs and attitudes will help reduce levels of anxiety.

Relaxation

One of the most powerful skills for coping with and managing anxiety is relaxation. It is at the very foundation of any program undertaken to overcome anxiety. Depth relaxation involves an emotional position that counteracts the stressed body state of anxiety. This emotional position has been described as the relaxation response. Some of the biological changes include:

1. Lowering of heart rate
2. Lowering of respiratory rate
3. Lowering of blood pressure
4. Greater alpha-wave brain activity
5. Lessening of analytical thinking
6. Lessening of muscle tension
7. Lowering of metabolic rate
8. Lowering of oxygen consumption

By definition, relaxation is at the heart of coping with anxiety. Depth relaxation techniques such as depth breathing, whole-body muscle relaxation, and visualization are distinct from more passive forms of relaxation such as listening to music or watching a movie. The practice of depth relaxation for 20 to 25 minutes per day will yield a beneficial relaxation response. Following only 5 to 10 days of depth relaxation practice, you will feel the benefits of the relaxation response.

Depth Breathing

Depth breathing involves breathing fully from your visceral cavity or from the bottom of your lungs. It is the reverse of the way you breathe when you experience anxiety or stress, which is usually rather shallow and high in your chest. This requires becoming more conscious of the act of breathing. Many people tend to use mainly their intercostal muscles—the muscles between the ribs—to regulate breathing. The average number of breaths taken is 12 to 14 per minute. Normally this number increases under physical exertion and decreases during sleep. The rate of breathing correlates to increased stress levels; however, breathing tends to become a shallower hyperventilation. This style of breathing is inefficient. Perhaps you have noticed how, when you are very anxious, even the act of speaking can put you out of breath. Clearly you are not getting enough oxygen. Thoracic breathing, which uses mainly the intercostal muscles and makes your chest heave, allows only for shallow breaths. It may also actually cause a certain amount of tension, as it requires that you draw your shoulders up with each breath.

Depth breathing has a positive effect on decreasing overall levels of anxiety. Regular depth breathing exercises also have been shown to be associated with certain long-term health benefits, related to cardiovascular and immune system functioning. Practice depth breathing by the following steps:

1. Place one hand on your stomach right beneath your ribcage.
2. Inhale slowly and deeply through your nostrils into the lowest point down in your lungs you can reach. Your chest will move up a little, while your stomach area lifts up, forcing your hand up.
3. As you have inhaled fully, count to three and then exhale fully through your nose. As you exhale, let go

and imagine your entire body getting limber, relaxed, resilient.
4. Remind yourself that all you need to do is give and take, breathe in and breathe out. Repeat depth breathing in this way for ten breaths. Concentrate on keeping your breaths *smooth*, avoiding sudden inhaling or exhaling.

If you start to feel light-headed while practicing depth breathing, stop for 60 seconds and then begin over. You may find that depth breathing will help to slow you down whenever you experience the symptoms of anxiety. Three to four minutes of depth breathing can alleviate even severe anxiety when you originate the breathing before it escalates. Depth breathing can additionally counteract hyperventilation problems. While depth breathing may seem somewhat awkward at first, it's a skill that relaxed partners utilize automatically. Depth breathing for a few minutes is an efficient way to reduce levels of anxiety, and it is always available when you need it. This may sound a bit technical and awkward, but soon you can stop using your hand on your chest and consciously switch to depth breathing when you need to. Further information on muscle relaxation and visualization in Chapter 5 may also be helpful in reducing your level of anxiety.

Physical Exercise

A consistent routine of physical exercise will help you to manage and reduce anxiety. Exercise provides a natural biological release of the adrenaline that accompanies anxiety. Physical exercise also relaxes muscle tension and initiates production of endorphins in the brain, generating a sense of well-being. Research has shown that consistent, moderate (20 to 30 minutes) aerobic exercise helps to decrease some of the neurophysiological imbalances associated with higher levels of anxiety.

To take advantage of the anxiety-reducing effects of exercise, it is best to do aerobic exercise three to four times per week for approximately 20 to 30 minutes. Aerobic exercises include brisk walking, running, aerobic dancing, bicycling, swimming, jumping rope, using a treadmill or stepper, and ice or roller skating. It is important to both break a sweat and raise your heartbeat for the above length of time. If you haven't done any type of exercise in a while, you may want to begin with walking for only very short periods (from 5 to 10 minutes) and build up your time slowly. You may find it helpful to vary the type of exercise you do. Variation can help reduce boredom and will assist in the exercise of different body parts. If you have any medical conditions that might limit exercise, or have high blood pressure, diabetes, chest pains, fainting spells, or joint pain, be sure to consult your doctor before undertaking an exercise program. Here are some helpful hints.

- Begin exercising slowly. Start out by spending only 5 to 10 minutes every other day for the first week. Add 5 minutes to your workout time each successive week until you reach 30 minutes. Doing too much too fast causes the greatest exercise attrition rate.

- Expect some initial discomfort such as aches and pains when you start out. These will disappear as you gain improved physical condition by applying an appropriate level of stress to your body and then allowing it to recover sufficiently.

- Warm up before exercising by doing some light stretches, sit-ups, and/or push-ups to get the blood flowing to your muscles. When you're finished with more vigorous aerobic exercise, cool down by walking for 2 or 3 minutes and do some stretches.

- Make a commitment to an exercise program for a minimum of 30 days and then re-evaluate. You may find exercise to be sufficiently rewarding so that you will choose to continue.

OVERCOMING YOUR ANXIETY 123

- Quit exercising right away if you experience any sudden, unexplainable body pains or other symptoms. If you go too long with pain, it will prevent you from exercising for a considerably longer time than if you stop and try again another day.

- Build toward a regular exercise program. The optimal benefit for managing and reducing anxiety will be obtained by working toward exercising aerobically three to five days per week for 20 to 30 minutes each day.

Time Management and Organization

The world demands much from us today, so that we must all organize our time at home and at work more efficiently than ever before. We spend way too much time looking for things, asking repeated questions, and just generally spinning our wheels. This simply adds to an increase in your overall level of anxiety. Organizing your life leads to lower levels of anxiety. Try any or all of these specific suggestions and see what a difference they can make!

<u>List jobs and their priorities</u>. If you become overwhelmed at all you have waiting for you, there is an answer. Make lists of things needing to be done and use it! Make note of when the jobs need to be complete and then put them in chronological order. If one of the items is a really big task, break it down into segments and tackle them one at a time. No one can eat a hamburger in one bite! If the things needing to be done are keeping you awake at night, keep a notepad at your bedside. When your mind won't relax and let you sleep, write down the things you are dwelling on. You'll be surprised at how committing them to paper frees your mind from needing to think about them!

<u>Organize your finances and mail.</u> Do you throw the bills in a drawer when they arrive? Or do you make piles for you to

get around to? We all know what happens. When it's time to pay your bills, you have to search through all the drawers to find them. Or if you have piles waiting to be read, you have a mountain of junk mail to search through as well before you find the bills you need to pay. Just a little time each day keeps you organized and in control. When you come home from work or when the mail arrives, sort through it. Scan the junk mail briefly to see if it is something that you might be interested in. If not, throw it away immediately. Even our monthly bills come loaded with junk mail. Open the bills, throw away the advertising material inside, and keep only the bill and return envelope. Create just one place where you keep your bills so you know where to find them. There are financial organizers on the market with pockets for bills and receipts, budget folders, expense logs, and so on. Find one that suits you. When you open your bills, put them in your organizer right away. Just a few minutes every day can prevent a mountain of work later.

<u>Keep a journal.</u> A daily journal can keep important things in the forefront of our minds as well. This journal can be where you make your notes and lists. There are many organizers and notebooks on the market (or again, you can make your own) for this purpose. The important thing is that you should always have it with you. Our most creative thoughts come at the most inopportune times! Your journal can also be just a place where you write your feelings so you can put them aside if they are keeping you from being productive. Again, it is really surprising how writing something down can free up your mind from dwelling on it and not allowing you to move forward.

<u>Organize and label your belongings.</u> We've all experienced the frustration of looking through a dozen boxes for something—it's always in the last place where we look! Seri-

ously, though, whether it's the attic, garage, storage closet, or office supply closet, you are packing it away for later use, right? Label every box with its contents so down the road you don't have go through a dozen boxes! It takes a little time but saves more time later. Want to go one step further? Make a section in your journal to log the contents of the attic, garage, storage closet, or office supply closet. Then you will really know where to start your search!

<u>Use driving time wisely.</u> Many of us spend a lot of time commuting to and from work. If you use public transportation or car pool, use this time to make notes on things to do, results of previous meetings, and/or new things you want to try. If you drive, use this time to listen to self-improvement tapes, music that elevates your mood, or the latest book on tape you've been meaning to read. You can also make notes into a personal tape recorder and then write them down later. Use this time to mentally organize your creative thoughts. Once you are at work or back at home, it's easy to forget these things as you go about your daily routine.

<u>Organize birthdays and anniversaries.</u> It is very embarrassing to forget a birthday or anniversary, but it's all too easy to do if you are not organized. We all lead frantic, busy lives. There are organizers on the market (or you can make your own) just for this purpose. They generally have twelve pockets—one for each month. On the outside of the pocket you can write the names, dates, and occasions that fall within that month (for example, "Mark's birthday, October 30"). Then use one of those cold January days to buy appropriate cards for everyone. Sit down and sign all the cards for the year, address the envelopes, put on the stamps, and put them in their proper pockets. Then on the first of each month, pull out the cards and mail them. Everyone will be

impressed that you remembered even though you are so busy! Don't forget to include this monthly task on your list of things to do each month.

Social Support

Getting support from friends, coworkers, or family members outside of a real relationship is a way to help manage anxiety. However, this itself can cause you a lot of stress and anxiety. Everyone dreads conversations where emotional and psychological stakes are high. But it is possible to have an honest, supportive, and anxiety-reducing social network. Here is an example of dealing with an anxiety-producing situation in a way that causes further conflict in a friendship:

Louise: "You are so stuck up! You are always putting me down in front of everyone. Did you have to tell Jason and Luann that I cut my own hair? You know money is a little tight for me right now."

Anna: "Your hair looks terrible. Maybe that's why you haven't had a date in six months."

Louise: " I don't think it's any of your business."

Anna: "Fine. I'm leaving now. Are you coming?"

Louise: "No, I think I need to trim my bangs!"

Avoid getting bogged down in too many details. Instead focus on the substance of what happened. Establish a fact pattern of who did what and how you got to where you are now. How would a neutral third party describe the situation?

Our feelings often get mixed up in our judgments of another person's behavior. Negatively describing other people's actions immediately puts them on the defensive, and they are more likely to stop listening and counter with a verbal attack of their own. This is a definite no-no when it comes to difficult conversations. It is much more effective to focus on how their actions made you feel instead of labeling their actions. In other words, replace the phrase, "You are so ----"with the phrase, "When you do X, it makes me feel ----."

Perhaps you feel vulnerable or defensive because some aspect of your self-image might be under attack. Identify which aspect of your self-image feels threatened. Is it your ability to make money? Your ability to sustain a healthy love relationship? Do you see yourself as a nice person who hates to put your foot down? Is it a trust issue? Figuring out where the pain or distress is coming from helps you to be more objective. And by being able to view the situation in a calmer and more rational manner, you are able to act on the situation instead of just reacting to it.

What do you want this conversation to accomplish? Do you want an apology? Do you need closure? Or are you trying to solve a problem? Deciding which outcome you are seeking will help you stay focused. We all know how easy it is to get sidetracked in a conversation, and this tendency is even more likely to occur when we are discussing emotion-laden matters.

Think about the situation from the other person's point of view. Again, this will help you to be more objective. Get the other person's feedback. Ask, "How do you see the situation?" Treating the conversation as a mission for understanding can also help start the conversation and will go a long way toward making it a two-way one. Here's an example of how Louise and Anna above might have resolved their situation more successfully:

Louise: "Do you realize that I feel hurt and embarrassed when you draw attention to my money problems?"
Anna: "I didn't think it was that big of a deal to you. You're

always telling me that things are tight."
Louise: "But I don't want the whole world to know. I only told you because I trusted you."
Anna: "I'm sorry. I won't do it in the future. Let me make it up to you. How about if I treat you to a movie?"
Louise: "Apology accepted. Just let me get my jacket."

Give the other person the benefit of the doubt. Perhaps it hasn't even occurred to that person that his or her behavior is causing you pain or distress. And, once you begin to talk, don't monopolize the conversation. You won't accomplish anything by making the other person feel taken to task. Finally, if a difficult conversation doesn't go as well as you'd hoped, don't dwell on it. How you handle a conflict is more important than the conflict itself.

Withdrawal from High-Anxiety Situations

Withdrawal is appropriate when your anxiety is Level 4 or above on the Anxiety Table. Staying in a situation when anxiety begins to get out of control (Level 4 or above) can sensitize you to a situation. Sensitization means strongly associating an event or situation with high levels of anxiety, so that when you reenter a similar situation, the level of anxiety automatically returns. For example, if you are with your partner while driving and your anxiety reaches Level 4, withdraw by pulling off the road as soon as you can, getting out of your car, and walking and doing some depth breathing. If you remain in the situation without reducing the anxiety level, you risk the possibility of becoming sensitized to driving in the car with your partner.

Work on letting go of concerns about what other people will think about your actions. Learning to withdraw is necessary to your recovery from anxiety and is the basis of time-outs used in basic conflict resolution.

Redirecting Attention

Redirecting your attention away from bodily symptoms as well as from fearful impulse-belief thoughts during the early phase of anxiety will halt the reaction from increasing momentum. Many people have found that the following techniques will ameliorate anxiety before it reaches Level 4 or higher on the Anxiety Table.

- Talk to your partner about your experience.
- Get some exercise. Go for a walk, ride an exercise bike, do some dance steps or other physical activity.
- Perform an activity requiring concentration like reading, going online, doing puzzles, knitting or sewing, or playing a musical instrument.
- Safely express angry feelings by pounding a pillow or hitting your bed, but do not ventilate anger at your partner.
- Engage in pleasurable activity, for example, get a hug, have sex, take a shower or bath.
- Have a healthy, nonfattening snack, such as a cup of decaffeinated tea with low-fat milk as a soothing treat. You will need to think of it as a healthy treat rather than a deprivation, however.

Affirmations to Reduce Anxiety

Use the following affirmations to help you regenerate a position of acceptance. You may find it helpful to repeat a positive affirmation over and over again simultaneously with depth breathing during the early onset of anxiety. If one affirmation gets old, try to find another that has power for you.

- *Anxiety isn't comfortable or pleasant, but I can cope with it.*
- *I can feel anxious but still cope with the situation.*
- *I can handle these feelings. They are only feelings that will eventually go away.*
- *This anxiety won't hurt me; it just doesn't feel good.*
- *This is just anxiety; it won't hurt me.*
- *This is just anxiety. I'm not going to let it get to me.*
- *Nothing serious is going to happen to me.*
- *Fighting and resisting this isn't going to help, so I'll just let it pass.*
- *These are just thoughts, not reality.*
- *I don't need these thoughts. I can choose to think differently.*
- *This is not dangerous.*
- *So what?*
- *This is not an emergency. I can take my time before making any decisions.*
- *This is not the worst thing in the world that could happen.*
- *I'm going to go with the flow and wait for my anxiety to decrease.*
- *This is an opportunity for me to learn to cope with my anxiety.*
- *I'll just let my body do its thing. This too shall pass.*
- *I'll ride this out because I don't have to let this get to me.*

- *I deserve to feel OK right now.*
- *I can take all the time I need to let go and relax.*
- *I can always leave if I need to.*
- *There is no need to push myself. I can take as small a step forward as I choose.*
- *I've survived this before and I'll survive this time, too.*
- *I can do what I have to do in spite of anxiety.*

Chapter 8

Overcoming Distorted Beliefs

You can't drive straight on a twisted lane
Russian Proverb

Distorted Beliefs Harm Real Relationships

Distorted beliefs are simply assumptions about ourselves, others, and life in general. Distorted beliefs also include errors in information processing based on unreliable thoughts and concepts, which can lead to dysfunctional interaction within a relationship. These beliefs promote negative interpretations of both partners' positive and negative behaviors and contribute to a couple's inability to resolve conflicts.

Where do distorted beliefs come from? We learned them from our parents, teachers, and peers, as well as from the larger society around us while growing up. These beliefs are typically so basic to our thinking and feeling that we do not recognize them as beliefs at all; we just take them as truth. Becoming aware of the distorted beliefs—as well as learning skills to change or overcome them with more logical, positive beliefs—helps partners to view themselves, each other, and life in a more harmonious, realistic manner. Here are some of the most common belief distortions:

1. <u>"All or nothing" thinking:</u> Insisting on black-or-white choices. This distortion involves perceiving only the extremes and failing to see the middle ground. Especially under stress, "all or nothing" thinking rigidly views choices as good or bad, perfect or worthless, competent or incompetent. Either the event was great or it was the worst event ever. In terms of self-esteem you're either brilliant or you're stupid.
2. <u>Shoulds:</u> Motivating yourself by insisting on what you *ought* to do or be, not what you actually *want* to do or be. The focus is on an internal standard based on what others think or need rather than what you need. The word "should" is a hallmark of the impulse-belief personality structure of a perfectionist, described in Chapter 3. Certain types of "shoulds" are a part of a healthy, normal concern; for example, "I should look both ways before crossing the street," or "I should not rear-end that car just because that driver cut me off." However, shoulds may also reflect excessively high or unrealistic standards imposed by yourself or others, such as "I should get along with every boss I ever have."
3. <u>Catastrophizing:</u> Perceiving total disaster as the probable outcome when you think about something that is somewhat challenging or risky. For example, you've been making progress and then you have a disappointing setback. Instead of seeing the setback as inconvenient and a normal part of life's ups and downs, you feel as though you're back at the beginning. Or you anticipate the very worst even when that outcome is highly improbable. In short, you project a catastrophe.
4. <u>Overgeneralizing:</u> Thinking in absolute terms such as "always" and "never." For example, on the basis of only one or two instances, you draw a conclusion about your

partner's characteristic pattern of behavior. Or you translate one negative experience, such as being turned down for a promotion, into a law governing your whole life, for example, "I'm a hopeless failure. I'll never make it in life." Or you have a problem in one store, therefore all stores should be avoided. Absolute statements such as "I'll never be able to trust you again," or "You always put me down," are examples of this distorted belief promoting a cycle of hopelessness in relationships.

5. Minimizing/magnifying: Minimizing involves downplaying your partner's qualities or the importance of an event. Magnifying is the other side of the same coin, which exaggerates a partner's negative characteristics or the consequences of a situation. An example of minimizing: Partner A tells Partner B that she is feeling very angry about an event. Partner B ignores the event and the feelings, hoping that the whole thing will go away. An example of magnifying: Partners have a disagreement over which movie to see on Saturday night, and Partner A thinks, "Now he'll be hostile to me forever. I should leave this relationship."

6. Taking it personally: A tendency to relate everything to oneself. Taking it personally involves the belief that everything people do or say is a response to you. Partner A scratches her head, and Partner B immediately believes he has done something wrong. Or Partner B snaps at Partner A, who impulsively reasons that it must be her fault. When you take everything personally, you fail to recognize that other people's negative behavior probably reflects their emotional state. It is grandiose to insist that almost everything is a personal reaction to you.

7. Affective (feelings) reasoning: The belief that you are

what you feel. If you feel guilty, then you must have done something wrong. If you feel inadequate, then you must be inadequate. If you feel worthless, then you must be worthless. The problem with affective reasoning is that feelings by themselves are not a conclusive definition of who you are. Feelings are temporary and sometimes exaggerated. They are important and deserve your respect, but they represent only one aspect of the truth.

8. <u>Ignoring coping abilities:</u> When people are either anxious or depressed, there is a tendency to overlook all indications of their ability to cope successfully. Positive experiences and accomplishments of the past are completely forgotten, replaced by anticipation of present and future insurmountable problems. The focus is on the problem rather than consideration of steps toward a solution.

9. <u>Tunnel visioning:</u> Focusing on one detail and ignoring the bigger picture. The detail of focus is typically connected to the present mood. For example, Partner A focuses exclusively on a disagreement that occurred this weekend, failing to consider all the caring and supportive efforts of Partner B during the week.

10. <u>Impulsive interpretation:</u> The tendency to misinterpret a statement or event by taking it out of context, ignoring pertinent information, and purporting a negative conclusion in the absence of any evidence. For example, Partner A learns that Partner B has given permission to their teenager to go to a party without discussing the situation with him. Partner A concludes that Partner B is intentionally punishing him because of a recent disagreement. Assumptions are often made without first checking them out.

11. <u>Labeling:</u> The assignment of a negative label to a partner's character or attitudes. The partner assigning the

OVERCOMING DISTORTED BELIEFS 137

label then proceeds to view much of the other partner's behavior as fitting into the ascribed category. For example, Partner A fails to make a telephone call during the day to Partner B. Partner B labels A as "irresponsible" and continues to see future behavior in that light, even if it could be interpreted otherwise.

12. <u>Mind reading:</u> Assuming that your partner knows what you think and feel without first checking it out. The assumptions may also include expecting your partner to know what you need or want without having to communicate it directly. For example, Partner A tells Partner B, "You should have known that I would want to go out for dinner tonight for my birthday," or even, "How could you not make dinner reservations? That was very insensitive of you."

Distorted-Belief Phrases

A partner's beliefs in response to a situation or event primarily dictate his or her emotional state. For example, two partners are caught in traffic while they come home from work. Partner A believes he is trapped and employs such belief phrases as "I've got to get out of here," and "How did I ever let myself get into this situation? I was an idiot not to take the other route." This partner feels anxiety, anger, and frustration. Partner B sees the situation as an opportunity to calm down, relax, and listen to music. He says such things to himself as "I can unwind by doing some depth breathing" or "I might as well go with the flow." What this partner exudes is a sense of acceptance and self-soothing. In both partners, the event is exactly the same, but the emotional states in response to the event are uniquely different.

Your belief phrases regarding a situation or event

generate your mood and feelings. Therefore *you* are primarily responsible for how you feel. At the very least, you are responsible for exploring the beliefs connected to your mood rather than blaming it on the situation or on your partner. Partners who experience moderate or greater levels of anxiety are especially prone to engage in distorted-belief phrases. It is through accepting this responsibility that partners will ultimately be able to take charge and have real control over their life. Here are some fundamentals regarding distorted-belief phrases.

1. Distorted-belief phrases are typically so automatic and subtle that you are unaware of them or their effect on your moods. You respond without being aware of what you told yourself.
2. Distorted-belief phrases often appear in coded form. One short word or image contains a whole series of thoughts, memories, or associations.
3. Distorted-belief phrases are often irrational but almost always believed. For example, anxious "what if" thinking leads you to expect a negative outcome, one that is highly unlikely to occur. Yet, because the impulse belief phrase is sent so rapidly, it goes unchallenged.
4. Just as you can replace unhealthy behavioral habits (such as smoking or drinking excess coffee) with more positive, health-promoting behavior, so can you replace unhealthy thinking with more positive, supportive mental habits.

Typical Distorted-Belief Phrases

The following are some typical distorted-belief phrases that damage real relationships:

- *I should always be generous and unselfish.*
- *I should be perfect.*
- *I should be able to endure any hardship.*
- *I should be able to find a quick solution to all problems.*
- *I should never feel tired or lazy.*
- *I should always be efficient.*
- *I should always be competent.*
- *I should never be angry or irritable.*
- *I should always be pleasant or nice no matter how I feel.*
- *I am powerless or helpless.*
- *I am a victim of circumstances.*
- *I am unworthy. I'm not good enough.*
- *I feel ashamed of my condition.*
- *I'm nothing unless I'm loved.*
- *I feel personally threatened when criticized.*
- *I don't have the money to do what I really want.*
- *There is seldom enough time to do what I want.*
- *Life is very difficult—it's a struggle.*
- *If things are going well, watch out!*
- *I don't deserve to be successful or happy.*
- *It's useless to bother.*
- *My condition seems hopeless.*
- *There is something fundamentally wrong with me.*
- *If I take risks to get better, I'm afraid I'll fail.*

- *If I take risks to get better, I'm afraid I'll succeed.*
- *If I recovered, I might have to deal with realities I'd rather not face.*
- *I can't stand being separated from others.*
- *It's very hard to be alone.*
- *What others think of me is very important.*
- *It's important to please others.*
- *People won't like me if they see who I really am.*
- *I need to keep up a front or others will see my weaknesses.*
- *My accomplishments at work/school are extremely important.*
- *Success is everything.*
- *I have to be the best at what I do.*
- *I have to be somebody really outstanding.*
- *To fail is terrible.*
- *I can't rely on others for help.*
- *I can't receive from others.*
- *If I let people get too close, I'm afraid of being controlled.*
- *I can't tolerate being out of control.*
- *I'm the only one who can solve my problems.*
- *I'm just the way I am—I can't really change.*
- *The world outside is a dangerous place.*
- *Unless you worry about a problem, it just gets worse.*
- *It's risky to trust people.*
- *My problems will go away on their own with time.*

Distorted-Belief Personality Structures

Distorted beliefs commonly determine archetypal personality structures that can thwart you through a negative distorted-belief dialogue. Four common distorted belief personality structures are the pessimist, the faultfinder, the victim, and the perfectionist.

The Pessimist

The pessimist has a distorted-belief personality structure found in many partners who are prone to anxiety. The pessimist's predominant tendencies include a) anticipating negative outcomes, b) fear of the future, and c) catastrophizing. The pessimist is forever hypervigilant, watching with trepidation for signs of trouble. "What if?" is a phrase familiar to the pessimist.

Instead of "What if?" you can say: *"So what?" "I can handle this." "I can be anxious and still do this." "This may be scary, but I can tolerate a little anxiety, knowing that it will pass." "I'll get used to this with practice." "I can retreat if necessary."*

The Faultfinder

Faultfinders have a distorted-belief personality structure that is constantly judging and evaluating their own behavior, pointing out flaws and limitations whenever possible. In order to highlight another's inadequacy or failure, the faultfinder pounces on their mistakes. The faultfinder typically uses comparison to bolster a favorable self. For example, *You should have gotten an A on that paper, like Sally. But at least you did better than Bob. He only got a C minus.* "You could have done better" is a phrase familiar to the faultfinder.

Instead of "You could have done better," you can

say: *"I'm OK the way I am." "I'm lovable and capable." "I'm a unique and creative person." "I deserve the good things in life as much as anyone else." "I accept and believe in myself." "I'm worthy of others' respect."*

The Victim

The victim has a distorted-belief personality structure that feels helpless or hopeless. Victims tend to believe that something within them is inherently wrong, deprived, defective, or unworthy. They always perceive insurmountable obstacles between them and their goals. Characteristically, the victim laments, complains, and regrets life's situations. "I'll never be able to" is a phrase familiar to the victim.

Instead of, "I'll never be able to," you can say: *"I don't have to be all-better tomorrow." "I can continue to make progress one step at a time." "I acknowledge the progress that I've made and will continue to improve." "It's never too late to change." "I'm willing to see the glass as half-full rather than half-empty."*

The Perfectionist

The perfectionist has a distorted-belief personality structure similar to that of the faultfinder, typically self-critical. However, the motivation of the perfectionist is less to find fault but rather to improve. There is a grandiose desire to be special, and an intolerance of the unspecialness of setbacks. The perfectionist is dependent on external qualities such as: a) being accepted by others, b) attaining money and status, c) achieving career success, and d) being pleasing and nice to others. The perfectionist perpetually experiences stress, exhaustion, and burnout, by way of achievement and the drive for acceptance. "I have to" is a phrase familiar to the perfectionist.

Instead of "I have to," you can say: *"It's OK to make mistakes." "Life is too short to be taken so seriously." "Setbacks are part of life and a necessary learning experience." "I don't always have to be perfect." "My needs and feelings are as important as anyone else's."*

Adjusting Distorted-Belief Phrases

Distorted-belief phrases are *learned*. This means they can also be adjusted to become mentally healthy belief phrases. This adjusting requires first becoming aware of the specific distorted-belief phrases, understanding where they came from, challenging the validity of distorted phrases, and finally replacing them with one or more healthy belief phrases.

Become Aware of Situations Likely to Induce Distorted-Belief Phrases

For example:
- All occasions when you're feeling anxiety
- Times when you've made some kind of mistake or have failed to meet expectations, and therefore feel ashamed or inadequate
- Situations in which you feel under scrutiny or criticized
- Times when you're angry at yourself or others

Explore Yourself

"What have I been saying to myself that led me to feel this way?" "Do I really want to do this to myself?" When you feel too upset to explore and adjust the distorted-belief phrases, allow yourself the chance to acknowledge and express your feelings. Then later, when you've calmed down and are ready, you can proceed with the following steps.

Relax or Distract Yourself

Interrupt the distorted-belief phrases by doing depth breathing or using some alternative method of distraction. The objective is to slow down and self-soothe. Distorted-belief phrases are so rapid, automatic, and unconscious that they can elude disclosure if you're feeling urgency or stress. In some situations, it may take 10 to 20 minutes of depth breathing, whole body relaxation, or visualization to soothe yourself sufficiently to be able to explore your distorted-belief phrases. Under less intense anxiety or shame, you will be able to do this step in a few minute.

Record the Distorted-Belief Phrases

It may be difficult to unscramble the distorted-belief phrases that initiate your anxiety, shame, or anger by simple reflection. It can be confusing to ponder what you've just been thinking. The technique of recording your thoughts, using either a cassette recorder or a pencil and paper, will clarify the specific distorted-belief phrases you made to yourself. This step may take practice to master. It's helpful to be able to distinguish thoughts from feelings. The best way to do this is to jot down only the feelings first and then secondarily the thoughts that led to them. For example, the distorted-belief phrase "I feel hopeless and inadequate" is one where thoughts and feelings are mixed. It can be unbundled into a particular feeling—"I feel depressed"—and the distorted-belief phrase that precedes such a feeling—"I am inadequate." Therefore you first ask, "What was I feeling?" Then you ask, "What phrases or thoughts went through my mind prior to my feeling this way?"

Confront the Distorted-Belief Phrases

You can do this by requiring direct proof of justification. Here are some helpful confronting questions:

- Is this the whole picture or just a kernel of truth?
- Am I being balanced in my thinking about this?
- What's the worst scenario here? Then what would happen?
- What evidence is there for this?
- What is the real truth about this?
- Has this ever been true before?

There are two helpful questions in confronting distorted-belief phrases, which challenge the rationale of such beliefs:

- Did I choose this belief, or did it come out of my experiences in childhood?
- Does this belief promote my well-being?

Affirmations for Replacing Distorted Beliefs

An affirmation is a short, simple, and direct phrase validating the positive humanity of an individual; for example, "I believe in myself." Affirmations work because they offer the user an alternative, positive belief phrase to replace a negative, distorted phrase. Several points are helpful before using affirmations:

- Use the most positive affirmations you can to replace old, negative distorted-belief phrases.
- Don't use affirmations in the future tense because it is important for your mind to experience a new belief *as if it has already occurred.* For example, don't say, "I *will be* able to express myself comfortably" but "I *am* able to express myself comfortably."

- Writing down or saying the affirmations out loud will produce a deeper level of knowing and believing than reading them to yourself.
- Repetition will also allow you to believe in a deeper way.

Here are some useful affirmations:

- *I am a worthwhile, deserving person.*
- *I am worthy of love.*
- *I love and accept myself.*
- *I am safe and always feel protected.*
- *I am unique and loving, loved and free.*
- *I am acceptable just because I'm a human being.*
- *I am healthy in all aspect of my being.*
- *Only I decide what success means to me.*
- *I accept my feelings and manage them effectively.*
- *I alone am responsible for my choices.*
- *I am successful in many ways.*
- *I have the power to forgive myself for past mistakes.*
- *I can set my own boundaries.*
- *I deserve support, and it's perfectly all right to ask for it.*
- *I am filled with energy to do all the daily activities of my life.*
- *I am at peace with all those around me.*
- *I express anger in appropriate ways.*
- *I am free to be myself.*
- *I am responsible for my life.*
- *I am at one with myself.*
- *I can trust my perceptions.*
- *I overcome obstacles to reach my goals.*
- *Each mistake I make is an opportunity to learn.*
- *My future begins now.*

Chapter 9

Mastering Basic Conflict Resolution Skills

A person can't be always defending the truth; there must be time to feed on it
                              C.S. Lewis

Why Does Conflict Occur?

Problems in relationships are more complicated to solve than individual problems. Issues of values, needs, and beliefs are not easy to resolve. Consider the budgeting of finances for a single person versus for two partners. How partners spend money requires the reconciliation of many differences. Even rather simple money decisions are difficult because old issues of difference are often raised, and unresolved conflicts may rear their ugly heads.

Research studies in human behavior indicate that conflict is inevitable in human relationships. Studies also show that conflict occurs more over perceived differences than real ones. In other words, partners anticipate barriers to getting their needs met that may or may not be real. Partners each have unique ways of dealing with conflicts in their lives. Coming to understand your style and motives, as well as the style and motives of your partner, will help you resolve relationship conflict more effectively.

Relationship conflict can become a power struggle or an adversarial competition. It is sometimes driven by either or both partners' needing to prove they are right, having a superior attitude, or desiring to hurt each other or "get even." The following are reasons why conflict occurs in relationships.

Lack of Communication

Failure to share ideas and feelings in an intimate relationship sets up a situation where the other partner may try to fill in the gaps. Partner A is left to read into what he thinks Partner B will say or anticipate how she will respond. Partner A may suspect negative things that provoke anxiety, leading to "looking for the worst." For example, if Partner B is silent at the dinner table night after night, Partner A may suspect that Partner B is angry or even having an affair. Yet Partner B may only be upset about something else, or preoccupied with solving a problem at work. If lack of communication persists, trust is diminished and both partners may become suspicious and defensive.

Lack of Effective Leadership or Decision Making

Lack of agreement about who's in charge or how things are going to get done in any relationship can be a source of conflict. For example, if one partner in a relationship expects democratic decision making and the other wants to be the authority, conflicts may be difficult to resolve. Then when other conflicts arise, the partners become diverted into a struggle over whose authority is going to be accepted.

Value Conflicts

Attitude, belief, and expectation differences may interfere with making decisions if partners are inflexible and hold rigid, dogmatic beliefs about the "right way" to do things. Different values and beliefs predispose the partners to choose different goals or different methods to achieve the same goals. And, since each goal requires an investment of time, effort, and some sacrifice, partners cannot pursue one goal without sacrificing another to some extent. Perhaps Partner A wants to spend money on expensive vacations and Partner B cares more about saving to move to a nicer apartment. Or maybe Partner A wishes Partner B would join her in attending every single soccer game that their son plays, while Partner B would rather go bowling with his friends some Saturdays. These types of disagreements can cause conflict in a relationship.

Gender Role Differences

When partners perceive their own and their partner's roles differently, problems can arise. For example, suppose that Tony's father always came home to a hot dinner and a clean house because Tony's mother was a traditional, full-time housewife with few interests outside her home. Tony may expect his partner, Amy, to live up to the definition of "wife and mother" he knew as a boy. However, what if Amy believes that since both she and Tony work full-time, they should share the child care and housework equally? Since their concepts of gender role are very different, conflict may result. Differences in beliefs about gender role should be discussed together by partners in order to increase understanding and tolerance.

Low Productivity

Accomplishing tasks and achieving goals is a necessary element of all relationships. When tasks are not completed, partners may become frustrated and angry. For example, when Partner A responds to Partner B's anger by finally performing the task, a destructive response pattern may develop. If Partner B's getting angry is the *only* thing that convinces Partner A to turn off the TV and clean the house, then Partner B will eventually tend to get angry right away whenever something needs to get done, because anger is the only thing that works. Low productivity in a relationship may induce manipulative criticisms and shaming interaction. For example, Partner A comes home from the office at 7:00 P.M. and says to Partner B, who is reading a book on the sofa, "You are the laziest thing on the face of the earth. When are we going to eat dinner?"

Change and Transitions

Change and transition are givens for partners in relationship. However, human beings tend to prefer secure, predictable patterns to the unknown. When transitions occur abruptly and without thorough processing of thoughts, feelings, and needs, conflict may result. Sudden changes—even if they are seemingly positive ones, like a better job—are likely to provoke annoyance, anxiety, and confusion if not adequately processed.

Unresolved Baggage

Unless thoroughly discussed and adequately worked through, partners' past unresolved conflicts inevitably have a negative impact on relationships. Many partners shy away from discussing conflict because hurtful memories of past conflicts remain. These past experiences become the baggage of our present. Relationships have the potential either to heal or to rewound scars from the past. For example, as a schoolboy Partner A came from a family that was always busy doing projects or working. When he would take a break from his homework to watch TV, his father would shame him by saying, "You will never amount to anything." Now when he comes home from working all day, Partner B may rewound that parental scar by criticizing him for taking time to replenish himself by listening to music or puttering in the basement. Or Partner B may help heal the old wound by affirming Partner A's right to take some time for self-care.

Distorted Beliefs About Conflict

There are several distorted beliefs that have impact on partners' ability to resolve conflict:

- <u>Harmony is normal and conflict is abnormal.</u> Conflict is in fact natural, normal, and inevitable whenever partners interact together.
- <u>Conflict is the result of personality differences.</u> The fact is that personalities do not conflict; partners' behaviors conflict. Frequently "personality conflict" is used as an excuse to avoid the conflict.
- <u>Conflict and disagreement are the same.</u> Disagreement is a simple difference of opinion, while conflict is more threatening. Disagreement is somewhat restrained and usually without the presence of powerful feeling; conflict is more feeling-filled and less reasonable.

Destructive Patterns

Because relationships have the ability to amplify the strengths and weaknesses in each partner's personality, conflicts can become a destructive power struggle. If the destructive pattern of conflict infests the relationship, both partners will feel angry, hurt, misunderstood, and rejected. Trust can become lost and the partners may fall into playing games with each other. These relationship games block the partners' ability to communicate fairly, and each sees the other as the one at fault and/or the one who should change. When this occurs, the relationship may become stuck. The partners reach an impasse at the same point in their efforts to resolve conflicts. For example, one partner may block any resolution attempts by routinely refusing to talk about it or withdrawing or sulking. This effectively destroys the conflict resolution process, and stalemate results.

Conflict Resolution Styles

Partners tend to develop one of four conflict resolution styles.

1. <u>Denial or avoidance of the conflict.</u> This approach emanates from the hope that the problem will simply go away on its own. Unfortunately it usually doesn't, so this is an ineffective approach.
2. <u>Giving in rather than confronting the conflict.</u> This style is typically used by partners who tend toward a passive approach. Sometimes these partners are being martyrs, sometimes they are fearful, and sometimes they are seeking appreciation. This is an ineffective approach for several reasons. It is unfair, it does not generate creative solutions, and regular submission deteriorates self-esteem and creates resentment and a sense of hopelessness.
3. <u>One partner getting angry and blaming the other partner.</u> It is as if the partners are saying, "You've hurt me and I'm going to punish you back." This conflict style leads to a stormy relationship in which each partner must win at almost any price. This is an ineffective approach because it precludes all constructive resolution, is manipulative and unfair, and produces lasting hostility.
4. <u>Seeking an innovative, fair, optimal solution for both partners.</u> This is the approach adopted by partners who want to create real relationships. Partners learn the skills required to control their angry and competitive feelings and their passive and aggressive impulses. They work to authentically find mutually acceptable solutions.

Basic Conflict Resolution Method

Partners who successfully create real relationships utilize nine steps to resolve conflicts of need. You and your partner may use some of these steps automatically and omit others if they are unnecessary for your particular relationship.

1. Recognize Conflict Issues

Healthy partners do not want to look for conflicts. However, when a problem does arise, you will find it useful to accept the problem as an opportunity to seek understanding of yourselves and each other. Think of it as a time for growth. Each partner's attitude toward the conflict issues will influence the creation of a solution.

2. Select an Appropriate Time / Place to Discuss the Issues

Partners need to select a context that will allow for adequate understanding and collaborative effort. When partners are tired, emotionally upset, or in a public place, or when they have limited time, they should postpone the process.

3. Treat Each Other with Respect

Both partners need to recognize that respect is conveyed by behavior. The way partners look at each other, select their words, and listen—as well as their tone of voice and reasoning approach—communicates respect or disrespect.

In the midst of conflict, angry emotions often turn to name calling or verbal attacks on the other's character. There is a descending emotional force that tends to move the level of communication toward disrespect during conflict. There may also be an inclination toward labeling the other partner. Talking at each other or past each other can become the rule, rather than talking with each other. An act of willpower may be required to resist the forces pulling you toward disrespect. Partners can use self-talk, for example, "I will not get pulled down." The assertion of a moral decision to treat your partner as a person worthy of respect is required, or communication will become no longer creative.

4. Listen Carefully

When feelings are strong and creative communication is difficult, partners are inclined to miscommunicate and misunderstand. Thoughts, feelings, and needs of both partners must be heard and understood. When partners truly listen to each other carefully, they begin to notice that they take each other seriously. Reflective listening is a helpful tool for conflict resolution in couples. Here's how it works: Your partner says something. You can speak up for yourself only after restating your partner's ideas and feelings, to his or her satisfaction. After you respond to your partner's statement, he or she then restates what you just said, to your satisfaction, before responding. Concentrate especially on reflecting back *feelings*.

5. Focus on Emotions

A key to conflict resolution is to attend to the emotions *first*. Try to understand what emotions your partner is expressing. There will be no resolution until both partners know that the other understands their feelings regarding the issue. *Listen until you experience the other side.* It is not enough to simply hear each other's emotions. The feelings need to be understood and accepted. If this step is skipped, there is unlikely to be a real resolution.

6. Verbalize the Conflict Issues

First each partner must get in touch with his or her own thoughts, needs, and feelings. When one partner is in the presence of the other's anger, there can often be a good deal of anxiety or panic. This may also be the case with one's own anger as well. The anxiety needs to be managed.

State your point of view *briefly!* A long dissertation will agitate your partner and may just be an expression of your anxiety. Be careful with loaded words! Words are simply representations, symbols with lots of meaning. They can be pillows or prods, comforts or bullets. But be *real* (authentic) with your partner. It is not helpful to withhold important information or talk about one thing when the real issue is another. State what you believe without going to the extreme. Tell your *feelings*! If you are angry or resentful, say that you are angry or resentful, or you have a lot of feelings about the subject under discussion. Until emotional issues are acknowledged, the substantive issues will probably not be resolved. Communicate what the truth is for you. Look for the connection between the problem as you see it and the underlying basic psychological need from which it might have arisen. How does each partner define the problem? What behaviors do each contribute to the conflict? What are the issues of agreement *and* disagreement in this conflict? Both partners must ask and understand these questions.

7. *Identify* Your *Share of the Problem*

Relationship conflict by definition means "we" have a problem. As each partner accepts some responsibility for the problem, both notice a willingness to cooperate and will much more likely be open to the discussion. Here are some helpful hints.

Choose one word to describe what you want to talk about, like "spending." Now state the word or subject that you want to talk about in one complete sentence, like "I'm worried that we're spending more than we can afford on Christmas this year." Be precise and specific. Try not to blame, ridicule, or attack your partner, and do not overload each other with too much information all at once. Take responsibility for the problem, and tell your partner the reason that you are bringing the matter up for discussion. For example, "I have a problem. It is a little difficult for me to talk about, but our relationship is very important to me, and by talking about it I think that we will have a better one. I think ___ is the problem, and ___ is what I am contributing to the problem. I would like to hear what you think and feel about it."

Statements like this are a healthy way to express potentially charged conflicts. If your partner approaches you in this manner, respond by saying, "Thank you for telling me. If I understand correctly, you think the problem is ___. I can understand that you think ___." Restate the problem to make sure you have correctly understood your partner.

Relationship conflicts may be the result of a specific behavior of the other person. Take, for example, a situation in which one partner does not pick up after himself or herself. The other partner may give this type of response: "I've asked you a thousand times to pick up your things! You couldn't be this way at work or your boss would fire you. I'm not picking up after you anymore! What kind of a role model are you to the kids?"

Compare that example to the partner who selects an appropriate time and approaches the other by saying: "Honey, I have a problem, and I need to talk to you about it, because it involves our relationship. Maybe I have not told you my real feelings, but I am bothered by our differences in keeping the house neat. I would feel more accepting of you and less resentful if I felt you were picking up your clothes in the morning before you go to work. If this were done, I would feel better and actually have more time to make the kids' lunches." Wait for response.

8. Recognize and Identify Optional Solutions

Partners have named their own contributions to a problem or conflict; it becomes clear that a behavioral change from one or both partners would be to the advantage of each. The next step is to agree upon a solution to the problem. Now is the time for brainstorming. Both partners should think of as many solutions to the problem as possible. These should be behavioral changes for each partner. It is important to propose more than one option because you will be more likely to discover one that both of you will find workable.

9. Choose a Mutually Acceptable Solution

Following the identification of the possible options, the partners mutually evaluate them and make a choice. The evaluation of each option should include (a) the steps in implementation, and (b) the possible outcomes. What will be required for each person to make a change by implementing a given alternative? How will the change affect the behavior of both partners and the relationship as a whole? If one partner prefers a certain solution but the other finds it unacceptable, discuss the reasons. Sharing your ideas can promote growth and prevent feelings of rejection. Continue discussing until you agree to try one solution to see whether it works.

Before Working Through a Conflict with Your Partner

Here are some helpful questions to ask prior to tackling a problem issue:

- Is the problem issue really worth the effort to resolve it?

- Will talking about these issues really improve our relationship?

- Am I willing to spend the necessary time and energy talking about the issue and helping my partner by listening?

- Have I chosen an appropriate time and place for this confrontation?

If the answer to each of these questions is yes, then proceed. If some answers are no, you may need to choose a different method of expressing your concerns (such as sharing feelings only, without problem solving).

Chapter 10

Learning Direct Communication Skills

"I need to do some office work for thirty minutes and then I'd like to spend some time with you doing something fun. Would you like to see an 8:00 P.M. movie with me?"

Clear and concise, this is an example of direct communication. This statement is preferable to *Are you doing anything tonight?* which does not let the other partner know what is *really* going on and sets up a greater possibility of miscommunication. "Are you doing anything tonight?" can be misinterpreted because it isn't telling your partner what your real thoughts, feelings, and needs are. It does not directly state whether you want to be together, do something fun, or go out to see a show. Nor does it communicate the time restrictions. Vagueness often leads to miscommunication and resultant conflict. Sometimes partners are vague because they are not comfortable asking for what they need or stating their position explicitly. Honest, straightforward talking sends a clean message to your partner.

Direct Communication Is Crucial to Real Relationships

Many partners have grown up in families where they did not learn direct communication. Direct communication occurs whenever a clear, concise message is sent and successfully received. When there is a lack of direct communication, problems such as misunderstanding, disappointment, resentment, and lack of resolution may follow. Without direct communication you cannot realistically expect your partner to know what you want, need, or feel. No one is a mind reader. We all require clearly sent messages in order to effectively respond. Couples get into trouble with communication when they assume that the other partner *should* know what they need or want at any given moment. There is an underlying, often unconscious belief that the other partner should be or is the same as oneself. (See Chapter 2 on overcoming the power of difference.)

It's hard to overstate the importance of direct communication because it is such an essential aspect of any relationship. Research has shown that couples who perceive themselves as effective communicators are more likely to be happily, rather than unhappily, married. Similarly, poor communication is reported to be the most common problem among couples who seek help from a marriage therapist.

The following Communication Experience Table shows a few possible communication problems and their possible causes.

Table 3: Communication Experience

COMMUNICATION EXPERIENCE	POSSIBLE CAUSE
Partner appears to be detached	Overly involved in your own communication, becoming oblivious to partner
Patner dilutes the impact of your communication	Weak delivery and poor organization downgrade the importance of information
Partner is impatient	You are not sure what you want to say or ask
Partner is bored	You are not being self disclosing

LEARNING DIRECT COMMUNICATION SKILLS

As you look at the Communication Experience Table, you may think about additional possible causes for a particular communication experience. There are many other possible causes. This is exactly the point; direct communication is very simple on the one hand and complex on the other. The sender may not be adequately sending a receivable message, or the receiver may be feeling angry or hurried, or a hundred other distractions may be at play. Any one of these distractions or poorly sent messages can cause a break down in the communication.

Direct communication assumes that both partners are psychologically strong enough and emotionally mature enough to deal with reality. The use of sarcasm, teasing, long-winded lectures, withdrawing, or pouting will work against direct communication. Partners are direct by letting each other know clearly what's going on even if it means conflict. This clarity also assumes being sensitive enough not to hurt the other needlessly. Let's take a look at the component skills and dynamics of direct communication.

Direct Communication: Skills and Healthy Dynamics

Direct communication is the simple process by which information is exchanged between partners. It needs to be clear and precise, and it needs to have impact. However, this exchange becomes complex if partners have inadequate skills or when unhealthy emotional dynamics create distortions. Partners communicate directly when the component skills and healthy dynamics come together. Here are some direct communication skills.

Attention

This skill is called for when one partner is talking. The other may be distracted or preoccupied and not stay with the communication. When appropriate, partners should face each other squarely; maintain eye contact; have a relaxed, open posture; and show that they are giving each other full attention. Communicating by talking on the telephone or when driving in a car does not allow for full physical attention, but partners can still listen attentively. Suggestions for attention problems:

1. Discuss the attention problem with your partner, being careful to model physical attention yourself and communicate in a nonshaming manner. For example, physically go to your partner and say, "I'd like to discuss something. I've noticed that sometimes we try to communicate with each other when we are not really giving our full attention."
2. Identify possible underlying causes of the attention problem, focusing on the dynamics between you and your partner rather than blaming only one partner. For example, "When I try to talk to you from the kitchen while I'm doing the dishes, I am disappointed in our conversation."
3. Brainstorm possible solutions to the attention problem, being careful to maintain a mutual approach to resolution. For example, "This is what I can do to make the problem better, and this is what you can do."
4. Agree with your partner on a resolution to the attention problem. If the agreed-upon resolution does not seem to work the way you hoped, it can be revisited down the road.

Listening

This skill is called for when one or both partners have the experience of not being heard. Partners need to listen carefully and thoughtfully when the other is talking by paying attention both to the words and to the underlying feelings. There should be a minimum of interrupting each other, mind wandering, or preoccupation by thinking of what will be said next.

Suggestions for listening problems:

1. Discuss the listening problem with your partner, being careful to do so in a nonshaming manner. For example, "I've been thinking about how we might communicate in a more effective way by improving our listening to each other."
2. Identify issues from each partner's past or childhood experience that may lead to an understanding of the present situation. For example, "I did not feel listened to by my parents when I was young." Or, "I was wondering if you got tired of your mother trying to talk to you about all her problems when you were the only one around after your father left the house."
3. Brainstorm possible solutions to the listening problem being careful to maintain a mutual approach to resolution. For example, "I could ask you for your attention first instead of just starting to talk when I want to discuss something with you." Or, "I was wondering if you could tell me when you are ready to listen to me so I'll know when you are ready to hear me."
4. Agree with your partner on a resolution to the listening problem. If the agreed-upon resolution does not seem to work the way you hoped, it can be revisited down the road.
5. Review Chapter 11 on the art of real listening.

Respect

This skill is called for when one or both partners do not feel respected. Partners need to let each other know that they value each other as people, that they see each other as unique human beings who have the wisdom of their unique experience. Partner A affirms Partner B's right to be in charge of Partner B's own life, and vice versa. Partners are on each other's side and support each other's growth. They let each other know that they want the best for each other. Suggestions for respect problems:

1. Discuss the respect problem with your partner, being careful to do so in a nonshaming manner. For example, "I've been thinking about our relationship, and I'm wondering if we have lost some respect for each other."
2. Identify some possible underlying causes of the respect problem from history of the relationship and also your individual past and childhood experiences. For example, "I think some of our loss of respect for each other may have begun when I had my abortion. I'm not sure we have talked enough about it together. I need to understand more of your reaction to it." Or, "I realize that I didn't respect my father very much for how he treated my mother. I wonder if that could have some impact on us?"
3. Brainstorm possible solutions to the respect problem as in example given in item 2 just above: "We could talk more about the abortion and our reactions to the whole experience." Or, "We could get help from a psychotherapist."
4. Agree with your partner on a resolution to the respect problem. For example, "Since it is very difficult for both of us to discuss the abortion together, we will set up a consultation for next week with a psychotherapist for help in talking it through. If we don't like the first psychotherapist we consult, we'll keep shopping around until we find one with whom we both feel comfortable."
5. Review Chapters 2 and 3 on overcoming the power of difference and shame.

Empathy

This skill is called for when one or both partners do not feel understood. Partners need to make it a point to understand where each other's thoughts and feelings are coming from. They need to "stand in each other's shoes" and experience the feelings of the other. They can listen to what the other says before expressing their own thoughts or feelings. They can check out their understanding of what has been expressed when they are not sure of their interpretation. They realize that hearing each other doesn't help very much unless they know what is meant behind the words.

Suggestions for empathy problems:

1. Discuss the empathy problem with your partner, being careful to do so in a nonshaming manner. For example, "I've been thinking about our relationship, and I'm wondering whether we have lost some ability to put ourselves in each other's shoes."
2. Identify some possible underlying causes of the empathy problem from the history of the relationship and also your individual past and childhood experiences. For example, "I think some of my inability to empathize with you began when you got your new position and switched companies. I've never had a job anything like that, so it's harder for me to identify with you now. I'm not sure we have talked enough about it together. I need to understand more of your reaction to it." Or, "I realize that I didn't get much understanding or empathy from my last girlfriend. Maybe it's still hard for me to believe deep down that you're not like her in that way."
3. Brainstorm possible solutions to the empathy problem. For example, "We could talk more about our reactions to the job change." Or, "We could set up a time each evening to discuss our day."
4. Agree with your partner on a resolution to the empathy problem. For example, "Since it is not easy for either of us to discuss our lives with each other, we will set up a time each week to go for a walk and talk."
5. Review Chapters 2 and 3 on overcoming the power of difference and shame.

Acceptance

This skill is called for when one or both partners feel unaccepted. The partners will need to accept each other the way they are. They cannot try to change each other's personality or behavior. Instead they must learn to believe that each has a right to his or her own thoughts, feelings, and attitudes. They may disagree at times, but they don't try to change the other's viewpoint. When one partner disagrees, they can make it a point to understand without putting the other down. When disagreements arise, the partners need not be defensive or argumentative.

Suggestions for acceptance problems:

1. Discuss the acceptance problem with your partner, being careful to do so in a nonshaming manner. For example, "I've been thinking about our relationship, and I'm wondering if we have lost some ability to accept each other for who we really are."
2. Identify some possible underlying causes of the acceptance problem from the history of the relationship and also your individual past and childhood experiences. For example, "I wonder if some of my inability to be more accepting of who you are began when my mother died and you didn't even seem upset about it. I'm not sure I've been able to talk enough about it with you. I need you to understand about my mother and me." Or, "I wonder if your mother having three more children after you came along has any connection to our relationship."
3. Brainstorm possible solutions to the acceptance problem. For example, "We could talk more about my mother's death." Or, "We might talk to each other about our relationships with our mothers."
4. Agree with your partner on a resolution to the acceptance problem. For example, "Since it is very difficult for both of us to find time to discuss our lives with each other, we will set up a time each evening to discuss our day."

5. Review Chapters 2 and 3 on overcoming the power of difference and shame as well as this chapter on direct communication.

Assertiveness

This skill is called for when one or both partners feel taken advantage of or resentful for giving more than the other. Partners need not suffer in silence but must not be bullies either. They can care for each other but put a high priority on taking care of themselves as well. They can express their own thoughts, feelings, attitudes, and ideas. They need not expect each other always to agree, but can expect the other to value what they have to say. They should refrain from saying yes when they mean no. They want each other to be assertive.

Suggestions for assertiveness problems:

1. Discuss the assertiveness problem with your partner, being careful to communicate in a nonshaming manner. For example, say to your partner, "I realize that I don't feel very good about myself when I don't express myself to you about what is inside of me." Or, "I am wondering if you are not feeling very good about yourself because you are all bottled up inside with thoughts and feelings."
2. Identify possible underlying causes of the assertiveness problem, focusing on the dynamics between the two partners rather than blaming only one partner. For example, "I wonder if something happens between the two of us that makes it hard for you to tell me when something important is going on inside."
3. Brainstorm possible solutions to the assertiveness problem, being careful to maintain a mutual approach to resolution. For example, "This is what I can do to make it easier for you to assert yourself with me, and this is what you can do."
4. Agree with your partner on a resolution to the assertiveness problem. If the agreed-upon resolution does not

seem to work the way you hoped, it can be revisited later.
5. Review Chapters 2 through 4 on overcoming the power of difference and shame, and developing assertiveness skills.

Self-Disclosure

This skill is called for when one or both partners feel that they don't really know the other. The partners need to be open. They can express their thoughts, feelings, wants, needs, and fantasies freely and spontaneously. They can be willing to talk about their own weaknesses as well as their strengths. They can even be willing to tell each other the things that embarrass them. They need to tell each other what is really going on with them.

Suggestions for self-disclosure problems: see suggestions for assertiveness problems above. Assertiveness and self-disclosure problems are often closely related but not always the same.

Cooperation

This skill is called for when one or both partners feel that decisions are being made unilaterally. The competence and intelligence of both partners need to be affirmed, respected, and taken into account. The partners can then work together on projects with relatively little tension. Both partners can share in decision making and responsibility for results. Each can be free to share opinions, thoughts, and ideas without becoming argumentative or defensive. Both can take part in identifying, defining, and solving problems. They can negotiate differences so that both get some of what they need.

Suggestions for cooperation problems:

1. Discuss the cooperation problem with your partner, being

careful to do so in a nonshaming manner. For example, "I've been thinking about our relationship, and I'm wondering if we have lost some ability to put ourselves in the other's shoes."
2. Identify some possible underlying causes of the cooperation problem from the history of the relationship and also your individual past and childhood experiences. For example, "I wonder if some of my inability to be more cooperative has something to do with my angry feelings. I'm not sure I've been able to talk enough about it with you. I need you to understand my feelings." Or, "I wonder if your sister's serious illness when you were both children has any connection to our situation now and with my being ill recently."
3. Brainstorm possible solutions to the cooperation problem. For example, "We could talk more about my angry feelings." Or, "We might talk to a psychotherapist about our situation and my being ill recently."
4. Agree with your partner on a resolution to the cooperation problem. For example, "Since it is not easy for both of us to discuss our lives with each other, we will set up a time next week for a consultation with a psychotherapist. If we don't like the first psychotherapist we consult, we'll keep shopping around until we find one with whom we both feel comfortable."
5. Review Chapters 2 and 3 on overcoming the power of difference and shame.

Intimacy

This skill is called for when one or both partners experience distance on a consistent basis. Openness and intimacy can go a long way toward creating a real relationship. Many partners fear this dimension almost as much as they desire it. Openness and intimacy include emotional and physical (but not necessarily sexual) closeness, self-disclosure, spontaneity, playfulness, and vulnerability.

Suggestions for intimacy problems:
1. Discuss the intimacy problem with your partner, being careful to do so in a nonshaming manner. For example, "I've been thinking about the emotional distance between us lately, and I'm wondering why we have lost some of the closeness."
2. Identify some possible underlying causes of the intimacy problem from the history of the relationship and also your individual past and childhood experiences. For example, "I think I'm feeling distant because we have not been spending quality time together." Or, "I realize that I didn't feel close to my father very often. I wonder if that could have some impact on us now?"
3. Brainstorm possible solutions to the intimacy problem as in examples given in item 2 just above: "We could find more time to spend together and be more intentional about getting the closeness back." Or, "We could get help from a marriage counselor."
4. Agree with your partner on a resolution to the intimacy problem. For example, "Since it is very difficult for us to find enough quality time together, we will plan a weekend away this month."
5. Review Chapters 2 through 5 on overcoming the power of difference and shame, developing assertiveness skills, and overcoming your anger.

Emotional Support

Each partner needs nurturing and support at least some of the time. Each needs the other for care, protection, encouragement, and simply knowing that someone else believes in him or her. Partners need this especially when they are fearful, hurting, sick, lonely, or feeling vulnerable. Insufficient nurturing or support is a frequent cause of relational dissatisfaction.Suggestions for emotional support

problems:
1. Discuss the emotional support problem with your partner, being careful to do so in a nonshaming manner. For example, "I've been thinking about how we are both having a difficult time being emotionally supportive of each other, and I'm wondering how we can improve the situation."
2. Identify issues from each partner's past and childhood experience that may lead to an understanding of the present emotional support problem. For example, "I did not feel emotionally supported by my parents when I was young." Or, "I was wondering if you felt emotional support from your mother when you were a child going through the loss of your grandparents."
3. Brainstorm possible solutions to the emotional support problem, being careful to maintain a mutual approach to resolution. For example, "I could ask you for support instead of just wishing you could know that I need it." Or, "I could offer you support during those times when I feel capable of giving some."
4. Agree with your partner on a resolution to the emotional support problem. If the agreed-upon resolution does not seem to work the way you hoped, it can be revisited at a later time.
5. Review Chapter 2, 3, 5, 6, and 7, on overcoming the power of difference and shame, overcoming your and your partner's anger, and overcoming your anxiety.

Compatibility

When one or both partners believe that the other disregards his or her values, the issue of compatibility needs to be addressed. Disagreements about values and lifestyle preferences are inevitable. A real relationship embraces these differences and discovers underlying similarities upon which to build a common lifestyle. The greater the differences in the partners' childhood background, the more attention will need to be given to the understanding and transcending of different values and lifestyles. "Values" and "lifestyles" refer to religion, morality, commitment to social causes, sex roles, parenting methods, choice of friends, use of money, and so on.

Suggestions for compatibility problems:

1. Discuss the compatibility problem with your partner, being careful to model physical attention yourself and communicate in a nonshaming manner. For example, "I'd like to talk about how we seem to have very different beliefs and values, and we each seem to think that the other's values aren't as good as our own. Does that seem true to you too?"
2. Identify possible underlying causes of the compatibility problem, focusing on the dynamics between you and your partner rather than blaming only one partner. For example, "I bet the fact that we grew up in such different backgrounds has a lot to do with how alien the other's values are to us." Or, "Have you ever thought about how our parents' divorces have affected our values?"
3. Brainstorm possible solutions to the compatibility problem, being careful to maintain a mutual approach to resolution. For example, "We could each go to a psychotherapist individually." Or, "We could discuss our backgrounds with each other, focusing on how our values became important to us."
4. Agree with your partner on a resolution to the compatibility problem. For example, "We will take an hour on Sunday night each week to talk about our beliefs and values and their background." If the agreed-upon resolution does not seem to work the way you hoped, it can be revisited down the road.
5. Review chapters 2, 3, 5, 6, and 7, overcoming the power of difference and shame, overcoming your and your partner's anger, and overcoming your anxiety.

Barriers to Direct Communication

Many problems can interfere with direct communication. Honest and open discussion of these problems within your relationship will help make both of you more aware of yourselves and go a long way toward developing a mutual understanding of each other's real needs. Five barriers to direct communication in relationships are playing games, colluding, distorted listening, defensiveness, and self-absorption.

Playing Games

Playing games includes the use of ambiguous, indirect, or deceptive statements. It is essentially any communication that avoids having to make one's motives, meaning, or intent clear. As discussed at the beginning of this chapter, "What are you doing tonight?" is an example of a statement that, while not perhaps intentionally unclear, does not convey the speaker's full meaning, especially if he or she already has a plan. Or another example of game playing is the infamous "I have a headache." This old cliché, of course, means, "I don't want to have sex tonight," and is misleading as well as an indirect way of communicating.

The use of games can erode the trust and respect so necessary for real relationships.

Colluding

Colluding is a barrier that requires both partners' participation. The partners have an unspoken agreement to deny a problematic piece of reality in the service of maintaining the status quo of the relationship. To create this denial, the partners suppress or repress discussion of the problem topic. Denial of a partner's alcohol problem is a standard example. The alcoholic requires the other partner to join him or her in denying the presence of a drinking problem. To maintain the status quo of the relationship, the partner colludes and accepts the agreement. The partners together avoid any talk of alcohol difficulties. In time the drinking gets more severe, the problems increase, and it becomes more difficult for the other partner to keep to the unspoken agreement. Colluding prevents direct communication because it denies what is real.

Distorted Listening

Partners may hear what they want to hear rather than what is actually said. Each partner has a unique frame of reference—categories of experience from which values, expectations, and attitudes influence his or her listening. Partners also experience emotional responses when they listen to communication opposed to their worldview. Uncomfortable feelings arise when this occurs. In order to avoid the discomfort, a partner may consciously or unconsciously utilize selective listening, distorting or simply not hearing the communication. The stronger the feelings, the more selective the hearing. Misinterpretations are inevitable and interfere with direct communication.

Defensiveness

Defensiveness is an excessive involvement with protecting one's self injury or pain. Partners tend to react defensively when they feel threatened emotionally or physically. Most people become defensive, for example, when they feel that they are being rejected, evaluated, controlled, or dominated in some way. Issues of power, status, wealth, intelligence, and sex appeal can elicit defensiveness even if it imagined rather than real. (See Chapter 3 on overcoming the power of shame.) Both partners can try to develop a communication style that decreases the defensiveness of the other while keeping in mind that perceptions and reactions need to be openly discussed.

Self-Absorption

It is very difficult to have a fulfilling conversation with someone who is exceedingly self-focused. Self-absorbed people will talk endlessly about themselves and their experience or needs and make it difficult to get a word in edgewise. They may even ask you for your feelings or thoughts and then quickly move the conversations back to themselves. While such people are listening, they are actually rehearsing what to say in response rather than listening carefully. The content of their statements is usually seeking to fulfill an emotional need deficit. The best approach to self-absorbed partners is to check out with them what emotional need they seek to fulfill and try to offer a more direct solution to the deficit.

Levels of Emotional Expressiveness

In most relationships one partner is more emotionally expressive than the other. Partners can also be rather emotionally expressive at one time and not at another. Couples often find that one partner takes on the role of being less expressive and the other partner the role of more expressive.

Dealing with Partners Who Are More Emotionally Expressive

1. If you realize that your emotionally expressive partner is upset, initiate a conversation about what he or she is feeling. Your initiative will greatly reduce the emotional energy behind the issue.
2. A key concept for dealing with an upset partner is called *container listening*. When your partner is upset, tell yourself to listen carefully in order to understand. For the moment, focus on absorbing and containing your partner's words and feelings, not reacting to them just

yet. It is very important to rise above any reactions to defend yourself until you have fully understood what your partner is feeling.
3. Suspend all interpretations of what may sound like criticism, accusations, and blame. Delay your reactions to anything hurtful your partner says to you, and focus instead on understanding your partner's words and feelings. You will have your turn at a later time. This will help your partner to calm down.
4. Listen for the caring message underneath your partner's words. Reinterpret the words to see the caring meaning. For example, "You are always working late and never help out at home." Reinterpretation: "I love it when we are together—I really care about our relationship."
5. Container listening in this way produces a sense of safety and protection for your partner. When your partner feels secure enough to share his or her feelings, the relationship will grow and prosper. It is helpful to realize that you partner's upset is a result of feeling emotionally overwhelmed or threatened. Your container listening will go a long way to relieve the pressure your partner is temporarily experiencing. Defensive reactions will only add to the pressure and escalate the upset. Let your partner talk to relieve the pressure, and keep in mind that it will be counterproductive for you to get upset in response.
6. Refrain from any impulses to correct misinformation. Interruption before the pressure is relieved will not be effective. Wait until your partner seems to be done talking and ask if there is anything else. When your partner is completely done and you don't know what to say or you can't say anything positive or nonshaming, simply say "I hear you." Be careful not to judge your partner's feelings. Respect for your partner's differences and feelings will help to diffuse the upset quickly. Your partner needs to be heard, not fixed.

LEARNING DIRECT COMMUNICATION SKILLS   177

7. Stay calm and unanxious by taking some deep breaths or other relaxation techniques. (See Chapter 7 on overcoming your anxiety.) If your anxiety causes you to react and become upset, you will have to go back to step 1 and start all over again. Focus on managing your anxiety while you do the container listening.
8. When your partner experiences having been heard and understood, you have completed the container listening task. It is now your turn to discuss your thoughts and feelings. Your task has been to understand, not to agree. You can now expect to tell your side with the same consideration as you have given your partner.

Dealing with Partners Who Are Less Emotionally Expressive

1. If you feel the urge to express your feelings about an issue, take a deep breath, relax, and slow down. Ask your partner whether this is a good time to talk. If you know your partner is preoccupied, delay sharing your needs until another time when he or she is more available and able to be attentive.
2. When you have agreed to a time that will be unpressured for both of you, begin at that time by telling your partner that you would like some emotional support and that you need him or her to listen so you can blow off some steam. You might say, "You don't have to fix this for me, I just need to feel heard."
3. Keep it brief. Tell your partner how long it will take in an effort to help your partner manage his or her anxiety about your emotions. If your partner knows it will be brief and that there is an end time to the conversation, he or she can be more relaxed. Explain to your partner that he or she doesn't have to say anything or make any decisions. You simply want to talk for a few minutes.
4. Tell your partner that you are not blaming or criticizing

and that you know that listening can be difficult. Tell your partner that you appreciate the time and that the support is important to you. Refrain from high expectations of your partner to give more until he or she gets more practice at listening to feelings. You can expect more physical help later.
5. Give your partner time to process what you are saying. Your partner can't read your mind. A few nonblaming phrases that capture how you feel will be helpful. For example, "I'm feeling overwhelmed right now. I'm not blaming you for it, but I just need to talk about it."
6. Communicate to your partner your sense of him or her as competent and appreciated. This will help your partner to be more open and attentive to your needs. Shaming your partner will have a negative effect on his or her ability to listen carefully.
7. If you are feeling critical and blaming of your partner, discuss the situation first with a trusted friend or professional to help defuse the power of your emotions. Criticism and blaming will not work, even if they feel good for the moment. *Your partner needs support in order to support you.* Lashing out at your partner will not be helpful.
8. If your partner seems to shut down, ask him or her to try to keep listening. Do not assume that he or she is uninterested; do not give in to your urge to shut down the communication. Don't give up and try again later. These skills will pay off if you continue to practice.

Chapter 11

Learning the Art of Real Listening

It takes two to speak the truth - one to speak and another to hear
Henry David Thoreau

Listening to your partner can be difficult. You may find yourself being distracted, zoning out, thinking about what you will say next, making judgments, or feeling intolerant of what is being said. I have devoted an entire chapter to listening because it is the most significant communication skill in creating real relationships.

Good listening skills will provide you with better understanding and more meaningful connection. Listening is a skill that can be learned by making a commitment to grow. It requires putting aside the expression of your own needs, thoughts, and feelings temporarily in order to better understand and empathize with your partner. Listening allows partners to see through each other's eyes and stand in each other's shoes for a glimpse of each other's world. It says, "I respect and care about you enough to really hear what it is like for you."

Barriers to Real Listening

Listening is both simple and complex. In simple terms, it is the ability to receive the message that your partner sends. It is complex because it is so much more than just being silent while your partner is talking. Intentional listening requires effort to "get it," to understand, to learn, to discover the difference over and over again. The following are barriers to real listening:

1. <u>Judgment and critical feelings.</u> This barrier to real listening involves distraction from Partner A's conversation because Partner B has strong negative feelings toward what Partner A is saying, or even toward Partner A in general. Partner B may listen until he or she feels critical about what is being stated and then focus on Partner A's character flaw(s).
2. <u>Mind wandering.</u> Many people find their attention wandering from time to time. It is not unusual for a partner to stop listening and "go someplace else" once in a while. When this happens regularly, however, it becomes a problem that needs to be explored.
3. <u>Fixing and giving advice.</u> This barrier cuts off real communication because one partner wants to jump in to fix a problem before the other partner has finished expressing his or her needs, thoughts, and/or feelings.
4. <u>The need to be right.</u> This barrier defends against feelings of not being special or perfect. If Partner A cannot tolerate being wrong, he or she may not only turn off listening, but become aggressive in warding off the threatening feelings of being wrong by verbally attacking, shouting, lying, or otherwise justifying criticism of Partner B.
5. <u>Shifting the focus.</u> Changing the direction of conversation when it elicits uncomfortable feelings is another barrier to real listening. Some partners consciously or unconsciously use humor to prevent the other partner from raising serious issues.
6. <u>Pacifying.</u> This barrier to real listening occurs when one partner cuts off conversation by prematurely jumping in to placate the other. The partner is so anxious about con-

flict that he or she becomes overly nice or agreeable without full exploration of the issue.
7. <u>Reading your partner's mind.</u> This barrier is destructive to intimacy because it makes assumptions without checking them out. Partners sometimes mistrust what the other is saying and make assumptions about what is really going on. Often such assumptions are way off base.
8. <u>Thinking about what you will say next.</u> This barrier causes a good deal of miscommunication and resentment. Partner A is so distracted by focusing on what to say next that Partner B's words and meaning fall on deaf ears.
9. <u>Selective listening.</u> This barrier is more subtle than the preceding one because some parts of the communication are received while others are not. For example, a partner may pick up only on the other's anxiety or anger and completely miss the rest of the conversation, which may in fact be more significant.

Real Listening

The good news is that you can begin immediately to become better at listening. Just being conscious of the problem and of the potential barriers, and making a commitment to growth, can produce measurable results. Real listening between partners is clear and private. The speaking partner tries to clarify the intent of the message by stating precisely what he or she is thinking, needing, or feeling. Both partners try to make sure that intent equals impact—that is, that the message the sender wanted to send is the message the receiver actually received. Learning the skills of summary, clarification, process, effective body language, empathy, reaching for information, and validation can enhance listening skills.

Summary

Summary is defined as repeating back to your partner in your own words what your partner said to you, in order to indicate that you heard and understood correctly. This is the most significant listening skill involving an interpretive response to a partner's serious comments. For example, "Let me tell you what I heard you say." or "This is what I think your are saying." This simple skill, when used with the intention of more fully participating in healthy communication, will result in clearing away prior barriers to listening and correct faulty interpretations or distorted assumptions. The use of a summary will also help de-escalate anger and provide a mechanism for focusing on the listening process.

Clarification

Clarification involves finding out where, what, or how you misunderstood your partner's comments once you have responded with a summary. Clarification may be used for any occasion when you are not sure whether you understand what was said and you need more elaboration. For example, clarification involves questions beginning with "Do you mean...?" or "Are you saying that...?" This skill increases understanding because it acknowledges potential and allows for healthy clarification. When a partner finds out that he or she has misheard or misunderstood some communication, subsequent clarification (with the motivation of understanding, resolving conflict, helping, or caring) fosters better listening and good will.

Process

Process follows summary and clarification. Now it is time to offer your reactions, thoughts, and feelings without being hostile or shaming. You must own your thoughts and feelings, keeping in mind that if you are in fact feeling critical, it is because the subject has touched off your own issues. You give a glimpse of your inner experience to the issues that have been raised. Process allows for added clarification of how you perceive the situation. It also gives your partner validation of the reality of the issues as well as a potentially new way to perceive the situation.

Effective Body Language

Effective body language involves the use of the body in ways that convey intent. There are two parts to body language: attending to yours and watching or observing your partner's.

The first part of real listening involves positioning yourself so that you can see and hear your partner. In doing so, you are signaling your attentiveness to your partner. In addition, you are sending a clear nonverbal message that you are interested in what your partner has to say. The following physical behaviors will be helpful in effective body language listening:

- Intentionally face your partner as you begin listening.

- Look at your partner's eyes and face.

- Use open posture (arms uncrossed) and keep your body unanxious.

- Move slightly toward your partner.

- Use your face to empathize with what he or she says.

- In the pauses in your partner's speech, say "yes," "um-hmm," "ah," or find some other way of letting your partner know you are with him or her.

The second part involves watching or observing your partner's body language: all his or her nonverbal communication. This includes facial expressions, body movements, postures, eyes, arms, hands, feet, legs, and whole body. Observing nonverbal behavior is of particular use when your partner's verbal and nonverbal behaviors are incongruent. It is also helpful when your partner's feelings are not being expressed verbally.

Empathy

Empathy is defined as identification with and understanding of your partner's situation, feelings, and motives. Empathy is helpful in understanding your partner's position more clearly. The belief that you both are just trying to survive physically and emotionally provides a foundation for empathy. Everything you both do or say—including the hostile, inconsiderate, outrageous, or illogical things—is done to minimize threat or pain and maintain safety. From this belief, everything your partner does is some kind of coping mechanism. Some coping mechanisms are more appropriate than others, and some are more destructive than others. However, they all have the purpose of providing survival of the self. When an upset partner experiences empathy and senses that his or her feelings have been truly heard and understood, the intense negative emotional energy is released, and a return to calm coherence results.

Reaching for Information

Reaching for information is a skill closely connected to empathy. Using this skill involves asking two different types of questions. Open-ended questions are phrased in such a way that your partner can answer in his or her own words, maybe several sentences, not just yes or no. You can use these questions to ask your partner to elaborate on what has been said—for example, when you do not understand what is being communicated or you would like to explore an issue further. Open-ended questions often begin with "what," "how," "when," " where," "why," or "who." Here are a few open-ended questions:

"What would you like for dinner tonight?"

"How did you feel about what I just said?"

"How was your trip?"

"Why did you tell your mom about this before you told me?"

Closed-ended questions are used to ask for a specific fact—for example, when you are trying to pinpoint an issue or be specific about an issue. Closed-ended questions are asked in a way that limits the possible answers. They can often be answered with "yes" or "no," or some other word or short phrase. Many closed-ended questions begin with "are you," "do you," or " can you." Here are a few closed-ended questions:

"Would you like a hug?"

"Are you warm enough?"

"Did your brother come over last night?"

"What do you like in your tea: lemon or milk?"

"Do you want to go out for pizza tonight?"

Validation

Validation is a very helpful skill also related to empathy. Validation means simply accepting, understanding, and nurturing your partner's feelings. It is to acknowledge your partner's unique identity and individuality. Invalidation, on the other hand, is to reject, ignore, or judge your partner's feelings, and therefore his or her individual identity. When you validate your partner, you allow him or her to safely share thoughts, needs, and feelings. You are demonstrating to your partner, "I will still accept you after you have shared your real self." Validation can include listening itself, a nod or sign of agreement or understanding, a hug or gentle touch. Sometimes it can mean being patient when your partner is not ready to talk. It can also mean helping your partner label feelings, or remaining physically and emotionally present for your partner. Here are some examples of validating comments:

"That really bothered you, didn't it?"

"That must have felt really bad to you."

"You look pretty upset."

"You seem worried [scared, troubled, annoyed, etc.]."

Validation of your partner shows that his or her feelings matter to you—in other words, that your partner's real self matters to you. Through mirroring your partner's feelings, you show that you are in tune with him or her. This attunement, a state of mutual feeling and understanding, allows for a deeper and more satisfying emotional connection.

Conclusion

Real relationships are important. They are highly prized by those people who have learned how to build and maintain them. They are built, not fallen into by accident or happy fate as suggested by most musical comedies. People who grew up in nurturing families have a head start in learning how to build real relationships, but the good news is that *anyone* can learn these skills and bring about a hard-work miracle, as mentioned at the beginning of this book.

A real relationship brings together individuals who value their own and their partners' real selves. The real self knows and expresses authentic thoughts, feelings, and needs rather than hiding behind a false self or playing games. Partners in a real relationship seek to nurture, encourage, and support each other in ways that mutually respect individual growth and the healing of past emotional deficits. They are aware of their own individual emotional deficits and those of their partner. They learn and practice core interpersonal skills, which lead to a resolution of different needs, thoughts, and feelings.

A number of key skills for building real relationships have been discussed in this book:

- Overcoming the power of difference and letting go of the fantasy that your partner will or should change to become more like you is an important first step.

- Overcoming the power of both conscious and unconscious shame is another significant part of real relationships because of the destructive and cyclical nature of shame itself.

- Learning assertiveness skills helps partners to express their real selves to each other.

- Overcoming your own anger and that of your partner is required to prevent communication from becoming stuck or spiraling downward and becoming destructive.

- Overcoming anxiety is also important because of its potentially damaging effects on interpersonal dynamics.

- Overcoming distorted beliefs permits partners to respond to each other's thoughts, feelings, and needs in a more realistic and healthy manner.

- Learning the basic skills of conflict resolution and direct communication skills—and, perhaps most important of all, the art of real listening—provides tools and a foundation for effective relationship functioning.

Creating real relationships is work that lasts a lifetime, but it may well be the most challenging and potentially rewarding of all human endeavors.

Appendix
A Brief Technical Look at Shame

A number of psychoanalytic authors have considered the major role that shame plays in the psychic apparatus. Shame is the affective response to a conscious or unconscious sense of failure and inferiority in relation to the ideal.

Freud's brief consideration of shame seems to be connected to his early attention to narcissism, self-regard, and the ego ideal. The ego ideal here was a structure created by the internalization of cultural values, idealized parental representations, and moral precepts to guide the actions and contours of the self. Shame became for Freud a defense rather than an interpersonal subjective experience, the latter of which was a reaction formation against exhibitionistic/sexual drives. Moving from his conception of instincts, he discussed an agency of the mind that was to be *conscience*, and to function as a watchdog to the ego exerting behavioral and cognitive control over the drives. This agency, which he called the *ego ideal or ideal ego,* was to be the forerunner of the superego in his structural model. Freud suggested that the *ideal ego* was invested with narcissism lost from the sense of original perfection emanating from the infantile ego and determined the subjective sense of self-respect (i.e., self-esteem).

Freud explicitly related the ego ideal to self-regard and to its dependence on narcissistic libido. The inability to love, to invest in an object, lowered self-regard and led to feelings of inferiority. Here Freud equated feelings of inferiority with the functions of the ego ideal. Freud discussed object love as a means of rediscovering lost narcissism through narcissistic idealization of, and investment in, the libidinal object. It is interesting to speculate that, had Freud not turned his focus to the Oedipus complex at this point, he might have offered a framework for an elaboration of shame as a central affect underlying narcissistic phenomena.

Jacobson was interested in feelings of vulnerability and failure in regard to the ego ideal. She related this to narcissism and destructive early objects. Jacobson noticed in individuals a tendency toward shame reactions and feelings of inferiority. She suggested that shame developed from lack of control and failure with some reference to penis envy. Anticipating Kohut, she indicated that shame frequently reflects deficiencies that the individual feels incapable of remedying. Passive, masochistic, and dependent proclivities are present in such individuals, which may lead to ineptitude, evoking shame and inferiority.

Spero suggested that shame evolves from negative ego ideals, those aspects of superego structure that never gain complete internalization. These superego elements are differentiated as introjects and split-object representations, contrasted with internalizations of whole objects attained through identification. Spero suggests that shame reflects unstable self-other boundaries, and negative and devaluing internalized object representations that have remained alien to self-structure.

Borrowing from Mahler here, Spero believed that self-object differentiation is incomplete in excessively

APPENDIX: SHAME

shamed persons, leading to the threat of diffusion of the self's boundaries by envy of the "observing other," thus impinging on the self's separate and unique identity. Introjects and part-object representations predominate over true identifications and therefore threaten the separate and unique existence of the self.

Kingston suggested that shame could be understood as a movement from self-narcissism to object-narcissism. Self-narcissism is defined as an attempt to maintain a stable, integrated, and positive self-representation. Disturbances occur in self-narcissism when the self-image easily becomes negative (i.e., narcissistic vulnerability). Object-narcissism represents a primitive object relationship in which self-object differentiation and boundaries are easily diffused, quickly leading to an anxious withdrawal from important objects to preserve the integrity of self boundaries, and a swift attitude shift displaying toward others self-sufficiency, denial of need, and indifference. Narcissistic disturbance has its genesis with early difficulty in differentiating from parents who need to maintain symbiosis.

Kingston described shame as a signal experience reflecting painful self-awareness and separate identity (self-narcissism) in the face of difficulty in relating to others. Anxiety from this self-awareness leads to a wish to deny need, dependency, conflicts, meaning, and imperfection. Shame then recedes with the move to object-narcissism. Like Erikson's formulation of shame/doubt, Kingston saw shame developmentally as the urge to live up to parental expectations that disregard or violate a unique personal identity, but that offer a sense of closeness, love, or approval.

The importance of the ideal self or ego ideal in these writings leads to the view that shame is an ongoing tension-generating dialectic between grandiosity and the desire for perfection, on the one hand, and the archaic self as inadequate, flawed, and inferior. This tension results from the realization of separateness from, and dependence on, objects. Thus shame and narcissism inform each other as the self is experienced, first alone, separate, and small—and again, grandiosely striving to be perfect and reunited with its ideal. Uniqueness and specialness may be imagined in terms of total autonomy/independence or worthiness for merger with the fantasized ideal. The internal desire for autonomy on the one hand and merger on the other becomes the primary tension. The therapeutic issue becomes how to integrate the two desires.

Kohut defined the self as a center of productive initiative, the exhilarating experience that "I" am producing the work, that "I" have produced it. The self is the center of the subjective, the experience of the attributes of individual identity. Kohut uses the term *bipolar self* in describing two chances human beings have at a healthy cohesive self. The first opportunity is through the experience of adequate mirroring by the early self-object. This entails empathic mirroring of the exhibitionistic grandiose self. The second chance for a healthy cohesive self is from relationship to an empathic idealized self-object. This requires the experience of acceptance of the voyeuristic idealization of and wishes for merger with the idealized object, by the idealized object.

Kohut says that shame arises when the ego is unable to provide a proper discharge for the exhibitionistic demands of the narcissistic ideal self. Thus shame results when the ego is overwhelmed by the grandiosity of the narcissistic self, experienced as failure. He says that the shame of the narcissistic individual is due to a flooding of the ego with internalized exhibitionism and not to a relative ego weakness vis-à-vis an overly strong system of ideals.

The shame-prone partner may be ambitious and success-driven, responding to all failures in pursuit of moral perfection and external success. Kohut believes that clinical healing takes place when a shift in narcissistic investment occurs. It becomes therapeutic as the psychoanalyst demonstrates acceptance of the individual's grandiose self. The individual shifts some narcissistic investment into the idealization of the therapist. Thus the idealization of the therapist and the subsequent working through of empathic failures transforms the individual's exhibitionistic grandiose self toward a more authentic self-esteem and progressive self-stabilization.

In most of the early psychoanalytic literature, shame was considered a defense against exhibitionism/grandiosity. The more recent thinking, however, views shame as primarily an affective experience from which defenses develop. Even when shame in fact serves as defense, its affective experiential nature beckons to be understood and acknowledged. Excessive shame is a genuine human affliction that often requires professional treatment.

Shame presents in various ways, often very subtle because it can be mostly unconscious. Seldom will individuals speak explicitly of shame, but may speak of the experience of feeling worthless, invisible, pathetic, ridiculous, or foolish, or of simply feeling poorly about themselves. Several modern psychotherapists have noted how defenses help partners in relationships avoid the discomfort associated with issues of self-worth, competence, and identity.

INDEX

A

abandonment	6, 117
abuse	3, 117
acceptable solution	157
acceptance	1, 166
acknowledgment	68
ACOA	23
addiction	76
adult	44
aerobic exercise	51
affirmation	121
affirmation of uniqueness	129, 145, 146
aggressive actions	85
aggressive communication	60
agreement in part	70
agreement in principle	70
agreement in probability	70
alcohol	118
alcoholics	35
alcoholsm	4, 117
all or nothing	37, 134
ambivalence	23
anger	33, 83, 87, 90, 152 153, 155, 187
anxiety	113, 148, 185
anxiety table	113
apology	127
arousal	85
arrogance	38, 47
art of low visibility	36
assertive	6
assertive approaches	68
assertive aommunication	59
assertive rights	62
assertiveness	167, 187
assessing relationship problems	12

INDEX

apology 127
arousal 85
arrogance 38, 47
art of low visibility 37
assertive 6
assertive approaches 68
assertive communication 59
assertive rights 62
assertiveness 167, 187
assessing relationship problems 12
assessment 9
attention 161
attraction 21
attunement 22
automatic reflex mechanism 112
autonomy 33
avoidance 34

B

basic conflict resolution method 153
basic mistrust 86
behavioral change 156
behaviors 85, 155
belief phrases 115
beliefs 84, 91
blame 85, 152
borrowed shame 55
boundaries 6, 18
brainstorm 163, 103
broken-record approach 73

C

caretaker	22
catastrophizing	134
change	151, 3
character attacks	91
chemical dependency	117
child	20, 22, 117
childhood	163, 164
clarification	71, 182
cohesiveness	25
colluding	173
communication	22, 148
communication problems	161
communication skills	116
compatibility	171
complementarity	25, 26
condemnation	85
confidence	6
conflict	147, 153
conflict resolution	187
conflict resolution styles	152
conflicts of needs	18
confronting	152
conscious	4, 85
contempt	25, 38, 42
content-to-process shift	72
conversation	127
cooperation	168
coping	136
coping response	86, 87
creating self-centered universe	39, 47
creative communication	154
creativity	6
critical feelings	180
criticism as manipulation	67
cumulative stress	114

D

decision making	19, 148
defect	31
defective	34
defenses against shame	19, 33, 34
defensiveness	52, 174
deficiency messages	35, 47, 53, 152
denial	33
dependency	114, 144
depression	7, 51, 112, 120
depth breathing exercises	119, 120, 144
depth relaxation	119
disenchantment	26
distorted beliefs	20, 63, 133, 151, 187
despair	7, 32
destructive patterns	151
destructive relationships	3
developmental skills	5
difference	2, 17, 18, 20, 21, 23, 147, 156
direct communication	159, 187
disenchantment	17
distorted-beliefs	115, 137, 138
distortions in thinking	6
distract yourself	144
domestic violence	4
driven lifestyle	117
dynamics of difference	2
dysfunctional interaction	133

E

early anxiety	113
education	19
effective body language	183
effective leadership	148
emotional expressiveness	175
emotional insecurity	114
emotional needs	9,100
emotional need deficits	4,12,22,25
emotional pain	33
emotional support	170
emotional threats	108
emotionally healthy partners	5
emotionally mature	161
emotions	85,154
empathy	164,183
endorphins	121
entitlement	88
environment	20
ethnic	18
exaggeration words	89
excessive shame	32,42,45
excitement	116
exclusion	23
expectations	143
expressing limits	96
expression of feelings	5
external causes of anxiety	114
extreme feelings	6

F

failure	31
false pride	38
false self	2, 7, 8, 186
family	19, 33, 51, 99, 150
fantasy	1, 17, 23, 88
faultfinder	141
fear	111
fear of abandonment	42
fears of being assertive	66
feelings	25, 31, 55, 60, 76, 85, 136, 154, 159, 186
feelings of anger	97
feelings of anxiety	111
feelings of rejection	84
finances	123
free-floating anxiety	116
Freud, Anna	34
Freud, Sigmund	21
frustration	116

G

gay	3
gender	18
gender role differences	149
giving advice	180
God	37
grace	28
grandiosity	38, 100
gratification	3
gratitude	28
growth	157
guilt	5, 32, 101

H

healing	27, 48
healing shame	45
healthy development	23
healthy separateness	95
healthy shame	32
heart attack	112
helplessness	23
heterosexual	3
high-anxiety	128
hopeless	144
hostility	86
human attraction	21
human development	4
human nature	9
humanity	28
humiliation	37
humility	28
hyperventilation	120

I

identity	50
impulse	25
impulse beliefs	84, 86, 90
impulsive interpretation	136
inadequacy	40, 144
incompetent	34
individual work	9
individuality	6, 18
infant	20
in-laws	19
internal causes of anxiety	115
internal monologue	115
interpersonal	24
intimacy	6, 169

intimacy problem 170
intimate connections 36
intrapsychic 24
isolation 50

J

journal 124
joy 116
judgment 6, 180

K

kernel of truth 145
Klein, M. 24

L

label 124
labeling of difference 21, 137
language 18
lesbian 3
life purpose 117
listening 77, 154, 162, 179
loss 6
love 20, 34
love's debris 20
lover 25
low anxiety 113
low productivity 149
low self-esteem 2
lungs 120

M

major anxiety	113
marked anxiety	113
maturity	4, 20
meditation	29
mind reading	137
mind wandering	180
minimizing	135
misfortune	6
mistake	143
mistrust	100
moderate anxiety	113
mother/caretaker	23
muscle relaxation	91
muscle tension	121

N

name calling	105
narcissistic personality	100
Narcissus	100
need to be right	180
needs	76, 102, 154, 159, 186
negative judgments	90
neglect	117
nervousness	111
neurophysiological imbalances	121
nonconstructive criticism	21

O

one-sided changes	9
organization	123
overgeneralizing	134
overprotection	117

P

pacifying	180
pain	6, 33, 84
painful feelings	6
paradox	27
parenting	18, 117
Parrott, A.	118
passions	6
passive communication	61
perfectionism	37, 47, 117
perfectionist	142
personal growth	27
pessimist	141
personality structure	33
personality traits	25
physical	19
physical exercise	121
playing games	173, 186
political	18
poor nutrition	118
power	6, 48
power struggle	150, 153
pretentiousness	38
primary caretaker	26
priorities	123
problem-solving approach	103
process	182
projective identification	23
psychic process	22
psychoanalytic	23
psychological	19
put-down messages	105

INDEX

R

rage	39, 47
real listening	179, 181
real love	20
real relationship	1
real self	2, 5, 6, 7, 8, 20, 29
realness	28
recovery process	15
redirecting attention	129
reduce anxiety	129
rejection	37, 157
relationship compromise	78
relaxation	119, 144
research	20, 91
resentment	100, 155
resolve conflicts	133
respect	34, 153, 163
romantic love	21

S

sadness	116
saying no	79, 96
selective listening	181
shaming messages	99
shaming relationships	28, 48
shaming statements	90
sharing negative feelings	79
shifting the focus	180
self	4, 24, 46
self-absorption	175
self-abuse	43
self-activate	6
self-care	45

self-care skills	116
self-disclosure	168
self-discovery	27
self-esteem	6, 14, 32, 40, 60, 91
self-hatred	41, 42, 46
self-neglect	43
self-perception	41
self-respect	48
self-sabotage	43
self-talk	86, 153
self-talk phrases	94
self-worth	6
sense of control	27
separation	111
separation/individuation	22
sex drive	19
shame	2, 14, 23, 25, 31, 33
shame-focused culture	33
shamelessness	39
shaming behaviors	55, 99
short-term goals	14
shoulds	87, 134
skill level	19
sleep	120
slight anxiety	113
slowing it down	74
smoking	118
social support	126
sorting	69
spending	19
spirituality	27, 46
spirituality of difference	27
splitting	24

statement of your position 76
stating your position 74
stimulants 118
stress 118
substance abuse 4
suffocation 112
sugar 118
summary 182
survival strategies 34

T

tantrum 104
tendency to humiliate 44
therapist 52
thoughts 25, 46, 60, 76, 133, 159, 186

threat of violence 3
threatening harmful consequences 105
threatening to leave 104
time 125, 156
time management 123
time-out 108
toddler 22
transforming bond 1, 22
transitions 150
trauma 4
treatment 55
trigger 85
truth 147, 155
tunnel vision 136
twinship 19

U

ultimate truth	20
unacceptable	25, 31
unconditional correctness	88
unconscious	4, 23, 32, 85
unconscious identification processes	24
unconscious introjection	24
unhealthy shame	32
unique self	20
unresolved baggage	150
unworthy	33
useless	41

V

value conflicts	148
values	18
venting	91
victim	49, 142
victimizer	49
visualization	93, 119

W

wholeness	4, 25
withdrawal	36, 33, 128
working together	9
worry	111
worthless	41, 51
woundedness	23